World War II Revisited

*A collection of stories told by
those who served in the North
Atlantic, Casablanca and
Normandy. As well as those
who served from Singapore to
the surrender in Tokyo Bay and
for a short period after.*

Compiled By

L. Peter Wren
LCdr USNR (ret)

Cork Hill Press
Carmel

CORK HILL PRESS™

Cork Hill Press
597 Industrial Drive, Suite 110
Carmel, IN 46032-4207
1-866-688-BOOK
www.corkhillpress.com

Issued simultaneously in hardcover and trade paperback editions.
Hardcover Edition: 1-59408-454-8
Trade Paperback Edition: 1-59408-074-7

Library of Congress Card Catalog Number: 2005928404

Printed in the United States of America

1 3 5 7 9 10 8 6 4 2

ACKNOWLEDGEMENTS

Because my book, *We Were There*, is the story of the rescue of the *USS Indianapolis* survivors, many World War II veterans asked why didn't I tell their story.

In this book *World War II Revisited* the events are written so that the reader is receiving a first hand report of the veteran's experience. The need to record their stories was urgent so following generations would know what price was paid for the freedoms they enjoy. Some stories are grim, some have humor, and others stand alone for their contribution to our beloved country. The author makes it clear he is the collector and narrator of stories that should not be lost with passing of a veteran.

The cover on this book is the art work of David W. McComb and is used here with his kind permission. Pictured in his drawing are America's best steaming before Mt Fujiama and telling the world "Peace" has come. The ships are enroute to Tokyo Bay, where on the *USS Missouri*, the official documents would be signed, ending World War II.

Destroyers were a large part of the victory but always in the shadow of the Battleships, Carriers and Cruisers. In McComb's art the "Fletcher Class Destroyers" were placed in the foreground of the *USS Missouri*, giving those "Greyhounds of the Sea" a long overdue recognition.

Help in editing was given by my wife Helen M. Wren with the foremat and design provided by Mark Spratt and Terry Spratt of Cork Hill Press.

Chapter One

Foreword

The Geneva Convention Rules

Parade of European Events
(Prior to USA's Entry into WW II)

The Secret Meeting

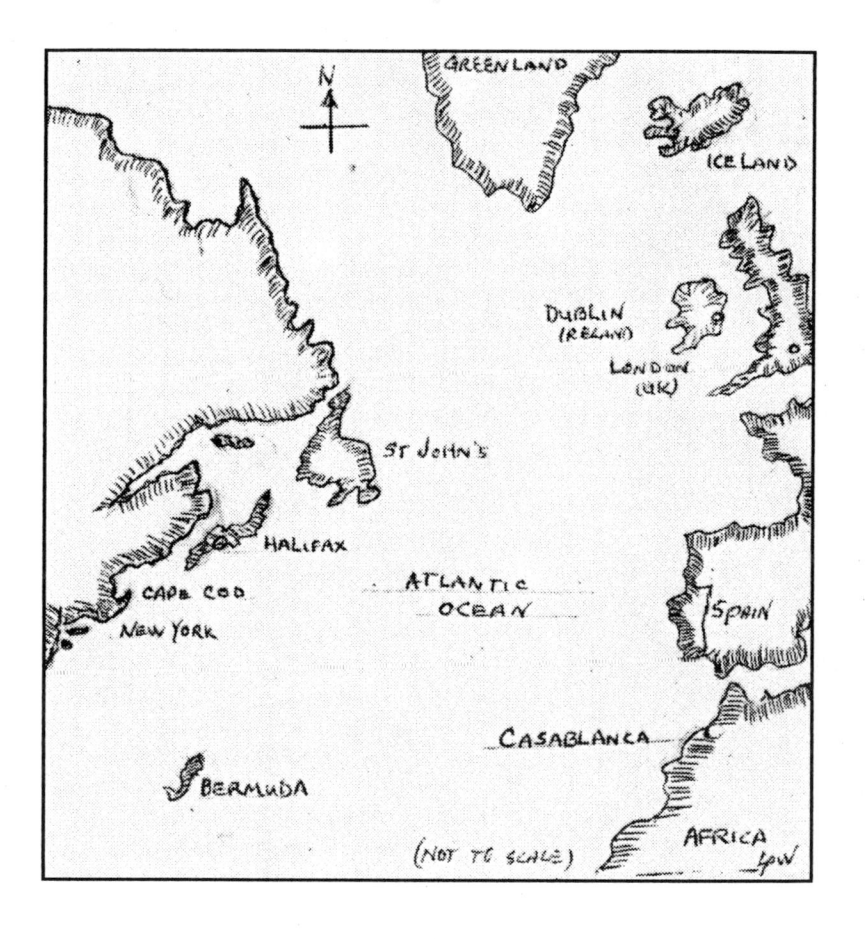

Foreword

The various writings in this book are an accumulation of patriot's military experiences. History textbooks record the dates, places and a brief general story of the wars fought. But it is the words of the patriot fighting from air, land or sea that poignantly tells the story of freedom won. There are times that will only require a pen, a book of laws, or a debating skill to resolve a conflict. There are also times when the Airman, the Soldier, Sailor or Marine must pick up his weapon, advance into battle and perhaps to die for cause of freedom.

Rapidly fading now are patriots of the twentieth century. They fought the wars through the 1900's. No longer will we know their stories unless they are captured and set into a book. Generations of children will grow up never hearing the patriot's story first hand. Let this book be one of those written to help them understand the price of freedom. May it inspire their proper action by pen, or by diplomacy or by sword to preserve the freedom that America has always fostered for all Nations.

World War Two was so named because so many Nations were involved. The United States of America entered this war on December 7, 1941 when the Pearl Harbor Naval Base was attacked by Japanese Forces. Shortly after that Germany declared war on the United States. German submarines were already attacking our ships in the Atlantic Ocean. American forces were spread between the Atlantic and Pacific theaters in this war.

France fell quickly to the German Forces and Great Britain stood alone to face the strength of the Axis Powers. America rallied to sustain Great Britain in the struggle to providing food, needed supplies, ships, aircraft, and military men. On the shores of Casablanca, the beaches of Palermo, Sicily, on Anzio, Italy and on the sands of

Normandy, France, America's sons did battle against an enslaving enemy. In the Pacific, America's sons spilled their blood on Islands never spoken before in everyday conversations. Today the names of—GUADACANAL, BATAAN, TARAWA, KWAJALEIN, BIAK, PALAU, TINIAN, SAIPAN, IWO JIMA AND OKINAWA speak of freedom won from Japan.

America dug deep into her deposits of teenage youth in 1944 and 1945 to replace warriors lost in the earlier battles. It was in mid 1944 and early 1945 when teenagers, still in high school, but with parent's permission were inducted into the military service. They were eager and willing to learn and do battle, and that they did.

Some stories in this book are grim, some very courageous, and others are humorous. But before reading about patriots, take a moment to learn the rules of the Geneva Convention which explains how POWs and captured medical staff personnel are to be treated. With this knowledge you will better understand the cruel, brutal and savage enemy the Allied Patriots faced in the Pacific War. All credit goes to the patriot who is listed herein. L. Peter Wren remains as the collector and narrator and nothing more.

The Geneva Convention Treaty

The Geneva Convention Treaty was completed and signed in 1864, and amended in 1906, 1929 and 1949. All European Nations, the United States of America, Japan and some Asian countries plus South American countries accepted the terms as were set forth. The purpose of the treaty was to establish procedures and provisions for—

(1) The care and treatment of the sick, the wounded and the shipwrecked members of an enemy country's armed forces.

(2) The methods of treatment of Prisoners of War, and Civilian population in the time of war was established. Also was the methods for identifying the dead and wounded. This information would be sent to the families of those persons.

(3) Also special protection was afforded to Hospitals, Doctors and Nurses who are **non-combatants**.

(4) All Medical transport vehicles, including ships, buildings and tents were to be marked with large "**Large Red Cross**" and not attacked.

(5) Other provisions were given as to the treatment of Prisoners Of War while confined.

In 1929 more provisions were added to the Geneva Conventions Treaty—

(6) **Prisoners of War could send and receive mail** which the enemy could censor.

(7) **Doctors and Nurses were exempt from POW status.**

(8) POWs should be treated as their own soldiers are treated. Enlisted POWs could volunteer to work and should be paid an amount equal to that which their soldiers were paid. Officer POWs were to receive the amount equal to

that paid to their Officers.

Prior to invading Manchuria in 1931, Japan withdrew from the Geneva Conventions Treaty. During World War Two both Germany and Japan violated the provisions of the Geneva Conventions. The sad facts on POWs treatment by these enemy forces revealed that **1%** of German POWs died while confined. Under the Japanese confinement **38%** of POWs died.

As a result of the enemy conduct the American Armed Forces directed any captured Americans in the future to give only—Name, date of birth, rank and service number. Further the captives were not to do or say anything that would cause injury to a fellow prisoner, or to do or say anything disloyal to the United States of America.

In 1954 the representatives of the Countries participating in the Korean War (16 UN Countries) and Russia joined again in the Conference in Geneva, Switzerland. The Conference failed to settle the question of unifying Korea and the withdrawal of all foreign troops, (Communist China). North Korea has been accused of rebuilding communist strength in Korea and refused to let the UN Neutral Nations inspect and investigate. This was a violation of the agreement. In 1958 Communist China claimed they had removed all of their troops from North Korea but they still will not permit the UN Neutral Nations to investigate. In 1945 Uranium Oxide was discovered in North Korea. Two rivers were dammed to generate electrical power which will aid in the manufacture of a nuclear power or bomb material. Question: If it is truly to generate electrical power, why is it so difficult to permit a United Nations inspection? Why must there still be a defense demarcation line on the 38th parallel?

Source: *World Book Encyclopedia.*

WW II Parade of Events — Atlantic

Sept. 1, 1939   Germany invades Poland.

Sept. 3, 1939   France and Great Britain declare war on Germany.

Sept. 5, 1939   President Roosevelt proclaims America Neutral.

Oct. 2, 1939   US Congress at the meeting in Panama establish a "Neutral Zone" extending 300 miles from USA Atlantic shores in which belligerent countries are not to conduct hostilities. The area is from Maine to Trinidad and will be patrolled by the US Navy.

May 12, 1940   35 USS Destroyers from World War One are re-commissioned.

June 14 1940   France surrenders to Germany

Sept. 2, 1940   50 US Destroyers are transferred to Great Britain because of the German submarine peril. In exchange USA received 99-year leases for bases in Bermuda, West Indies and Newfoundland.

March 27, 1941   ABC-Staff Agreement. America, Britain, Canada agree in event US enters the war, all will cooperate in the defeat of Germany. Also US will aid in convoying to the mid-Atlantic Ocean.

Aug. 09, 1941   Argentia Conference

Sept. 04, 1941   Destroyer *USS Greer* has incident with German Submarine. President Roosevelt authorizes any US ship threatened to "shoot on sight!"

Sept. 17, 1941   Begin convoy aid—British to meet at "Mid-Ocean-Meeting Point" with American escort vessels.

Oct. 17, 1941	Destroyer *USS Kearney* struck by German torpedo but not sunk. Occurred off Greenland and eleven crewmembers were killed.
Oct 30, 1941	*USS Saleno* (AO 20) torpedoed in mid-Atlantic but not sunk. Reached a harbor in USA.
Oct. 31 1941	Destroyer *USS Reuben James* sunk off Halifax Nova Scotia
Dec. 7, 1941	Japan strikes Pearl Harbor. FDR declares war on Japan.
Dec. 11, 1941	Germany and Italy declare war on USA.

Source: *World Book*, 1968
American Naval History, Jack Sweetman, 1991

The Secret Meeting

It was a meeting of utmost secrecy. It occurred on August 9th, 1941 in the waters off Argentia, Newfoundland. President Franklin D. Roosevelt, aboard the *USS Augusta* (CA 31), awaited the arrival of the British Battleship, *HMS Prince of Wales*, bringing Winston Churchill to this North Atlantic area. The reason for the meeting was to discuss the German submarines menace now on the trade lanes of the North Atlantic and help in moving British Forces to outlying colonies. The German Submarine Forces were attacking merchant ships transporting goods to American ports as well as those merchant ships bound for British ports. Great Britain, an island nation, was very dependent on their ocean transports and could not withstand any interruptions in the flow of supplies.

Winston Churchill stated it very succinctly when he said, *"Sea power was unquestionably Britain's life line. Two thirds of its food was imported. Transferring troops to the Empire's Foreign Ports depended on British ships to keep the lands from being invaded. The ships of the Royal Navy are all we have. On them floated the might, majesty, dominion and power of the British Empire. If you opened the "sea cocks" and let them sink, the British Empire would disappear with their sinking."*

So this is the urgency of the rendezvous of President Roosevelt and Winston Churchill. The meeting established the "Atlantic Charter" in which it was agreed, among other provisions, that the US Navy would secretly help transport 20,000 British troops to the Middle East to reinforce the India-Burma area in view of the threat of the Japanese invasion into the Malayan States. The British Colony of Singapore, "The Gibraltar of the East," must continue to stand opposing the Japanese threat.

On the date of the secret meeting (August 9, 1941) the United States was not involved in the wars now ensuing in the European and Asian continents. Prior to this Germany had invaded Poland and the low countries of Europe in 1939. Japan had invaded Manchuria in 1931 and China in 1937. When France surrendered in 1940 to Germany, the Japanese Forces moved quickly through China toward French Indo-China. This last action by the Japanese posed a serious threat to the Singapore Colony.

While the war raged in Europe and the Orient, the American citizens felt they were safe from these wars because of the oceans that buffered each side of our country. The "I" and "N" words spoken then were "Isolation" and "Neutrality." Many Americans felt the oceans washing our shores, isolated us from the ensuing wars and that we should remain neutral in all this conflict. If either the Japanese or the Germans had learned of this "secret meeting," it would have been deemed as a belligerent act and would have placed the United States into the Second World War in early August, 1941 rather than after the attack on Pearl Harbor on December 7, 1941.

With the meeting of the Statesmen a secret agreement was completed. Great Britain needed to transfer troops to the India-Burma area but lacked ships. American would provide the ships to effect the transfer of the British troops. The transfer was carefully begun on November 3, 1941. The plan would involve the American escorting warships and the troop transports. The three were regular US Navy transports, namely the *USS Orizaba* (AP24), the *USS Leonard Wood* (AP 25) and the *USS Joseph E. Dickman* (AP26). The amount of men to be transferred however required more ships. So from the United States Lines three of their merchant vessels were commandeered to accomplish this mission. The *SS Washington* became the *USS Wakefield* (AP 21), *the SS Manhattan* became the *USS Mount Vernon* (AP22) and *the SS America* became the *USS West Point* (AP23). The well-kept secret of convoy's destination was quickly changed from

India-Burma to Singapore after the December 7, 1941 attack on Pearl Harbor.

The convoy moving slowly and secretly was approaching the waters near Singapore between the dates 26th and 28th of January 1942. They came under heavy Japanese air bombardment in Singapore Strait as the transports unloaded the British troops. The last two transports to be unloaded were the *USS Wakefield*, formerly *SS Washington*, (slightly damaged) and the *USS West Point*, formerly *SS America*, both escaped from Singapore Harbor without revealing their true names.

Approximately 16 days later on 13 February 1942 Lieutenant General Arthur E. Percival, United Kingdom Army, surrendered to the Japanese General Yamashita a force of over 85,000 men. The Singapore Fortress and Airport, Britain's proud symbols on the Malayan Peninsula, were now under Japanese control. The British Colony of Singapore is a City on an Island of the same name and is just three quarters of a mile from the Malayan peninsula.

The Japanese main reason for capturing the many Islands and territories in the South Western Pacific, as they expressed it, was to prevent the spread of colonization. Once in control of these Islands and Malayan countries Japan would have a continuous flow of products needed for the Japanese homeland's survival. The Japanese Emperor and War Lords were convinced that the American interests in the Philippines and Guam and the English colonization must be curtailed.

With the above background now learn about the "Home Fleet."

Source: Proceedings, Naval Institute, July 2002
Naval Institute History of *USS Augusta* (CA- 31)
Naval History Magazine, February 2004

Chapter Two

Ensign Carter Talman Reports Aboard the *USS Wichita*
(CA 45)

Ensign Talman Meets Mr. Churchill

Ensign Talman at Casablanca

The Diary – by Ed Black

Julian B. Jacobs' Captured Spy

Three Landings – No Band-Aids
Robert A Stansbury GM 1c USNR

Ensign Carter Talman's Reports Aboard the
USS Wichita (CA 45)

Having completed a small book on the Confederate Navy I received a telephone call from Carter Talman asking me to drop off a copy of my book and pick up a copy of his book on the *USS Wichita* an American Cruiser in WW II. The source of these stories is from his *Memoirs of WWII* which have been condensed and edited and with permission granted to make them part of this book. His stories follow.

Carter Talman graduated from the University of Virginia in the spring of 1940. The War in Europe was having its effect on the United States. After Pearl Harbor on December 7th, 1941, there was no question as to where one's allegiance should be directed. Carter was selected to attend the Midshipman school in Chicago, Illinois and was commissioned an Ensign in the USNR on May 12, 1942. After a short leave Ensign Carter Talman is ordered to report to the *USS Wichita*, (CA 45). This is a heavy cruiser and operating with the Atlantic Fleet.

Some background is needed at this point to set the scene of what is now ensuing in the Atlantic Ocean. The German submarines and their warships afloat are endeavoring to shut down the transportation of supplies to the island nation of Great Britain or The United Kingdom (UK). In April 1942 Franklin D. Roosevelt, President of the United States of America, assigned a group of American ships to aid the UK in the patrolling the Atlantic Ocean. The division of ships assigned included a battleship, a cruiser and many old four piper destroyers. These ships are attached to the UK Home Fleet under the command of High Admiral Tovey.

Because the *USS Wichita* is on the Atlantic Ocean there

is some delay in Ensign Talman's reporting aboard. On 12 July 1942 or fifty-nine days after his commissioning he finds himself aboard the USS *Wichita* with a group of Ensigns all Naval Academy graduates. The patrol was near the Artic Circle and not far from the fjords of Norway. The fjords are deep and somewhat hidden making them an ideal location for the German submarines to sally forth and play havoc on the shipping lanes to the United Kingdom. The German Battleship Tirpitz is also sheltered in one of these fjords.

On July 14, Ensign Talman is standing his first watch on the bridge of this ship as a back-up lookout. In the operation plan with the "UK" the US Naval ships are on course 050 at 16 knots and fully exposed to the German Navy hidden in the fjords. The UK ships are laying back just over the horizon with the hope the German Fleet will emerge from the fjords and engage the American Fleet sailing so slowly before them. The American ships are acting as the "bait" to draw the Germans out of their hiding. When and if this occurs the "UK ships" will quickly close the gap and join the American fleet engaging the German enemy in heavy battle.

Well, the Germans do not take the "bait." While searching seaward intensely lookout Ensign Talman, calls out, *"Periscope, 2000 yards on the starboard beam!"* An American Destroyer is dispatched to investigate and it reports back it is receiving a solid metal echo on its sonar gear. Two other American Destroyers are dispatched to the area setting up coordinated attacks. In this plan one ship searches and listens to the sonar echoes and plots the submarines course, speed and depth. Then by radio directs another silent running Destroyer, over the target submarine and at the proper moment the silent Destroyer will drop its pattern of charges. Then the ships reverse the procedure. The tracking Destroyer becomes the attacking silent running Destroyer and the attacking Destroyer now does the pinging, training and listening ship relaying the information to the silent destroyer so it can drop its pattern of charges. The coodinated attacks are successful for suddenly there is a large black cigar shaped hull rising 15 feet from the sea. Then as quickly as it rose it disappears in the bubbling sea. Scratch one German Submarine. Ensign Talman's attentive eye while on watch garnered him favorable comments on his officer fitness report for that quarter.

Source: All stories on the *USS Wichita* were from Carter Talman's *Memoirs of World War II Highlights of the USS Wichita* (CA 45). Edited by L. Peter Wren

Back-up Lookout Talman's sharp sights German periscope and an escorting Destroyer sends it to the bottom of the Sea

Ensign Talman Meets Mr. Churchill

While assigned to the British Home Fleet, the *USS Wichita* developed a very severe vibration with the rotation of the starboard propeller shaft. The source was unknown but it was surmised that it could have been caused by being hit by a German torpedo that failed to explode or the ship struck and underwater iceberg. The speed of the *USS Wichita* was hampered in fleet maneuvers and so the ship is ordered to the "UK" Navy Repair Yard in Scotland near Edinburgh.

The estimated time to repair the starboard strut which was the cause of the vibrations would be 19 days. This is just enough time to allow each of the four watches a short leave in London. Ensign Talman's group includes the three Naval Academy graduates and upon arrival in London they engage a cab driver to show them the sights of London.

There were several stops and places to see but the most interesting spot was the "Changing of the Guard in Buckingham Palace." Unknown to them was the order from King George for the Guard to render full Military Honors whenever any US Naval Officers appeared at the gates of Buckingham Palace. Well, the timing of the Cab driver was excellent and the four Ensigns were watching the "Changing of the Guard" through the iron gate of Buckingham Palace. The Officer commanding the Guard, spotted the American Ensigns and changed the direction of the marching directly toward them peeking through the iron gate fence. After coming to a full halt directly in front of the Ensigns, a full honoring Royal salute was given and held, awaiting a return of the salute. The Ensigns were a little startled and embarrassed and not knowing what to do, they scurried back to the cabby asking him what was that last maneuver the Guard had just executed. The Cabby told them they had just received the full Honors Royal Salute and they should returned it and not scurried back to the cab. It was a nicety that King George had ordered rendered to American Naval Officers and they should return the salute out of courtesy.

The next stop was at 10 Downing Street and the guard on duty was telling the Ensigns that visiting hours were over at 4:00 o'clock and it was now 4:10 p.m. With that a voice came from within 10 Downing Street called out asking, *"Who is there?"* The guard answered, *"Four American Ensigns!"* With that the voice called out again saying, *"Send them up!"* At the top of the stairs was Mr. Winston Churchill who conducted a personal tour of his living quarters for the Ensigns. At 5:00 p.m. Mr Churchill announced, *"It was time for a 'Tot' for all hands around!"* They enjoyed a 'Tot' with him while he quizzed the Ensigns about their assignments with the "Home Fleet" under the command of Fleet Admiral Tovey. At 6:00 p.m. he dismissed them.

Guard: "It is 4:00 pm Sorry, but we are closed."

W. Churchill: "Who is there?"

Guard: "Three American Officers."

W. Churchill: "Send them up!"

W. Churchill: "Welcome, Let me show you around."

W. Churchill: "By Jove! It is time for a toddy. Will you join me?"

The Ensigns: "Yes Sir! We would be most appreciative!"

On August 15, 1942 the *USS Wichita* was ready to depart the UK Ship Repair Yard. Home Fleet Admiral Tovey and Winston Churchill were expected to visit before the ship departed the yard. The dignitaries arrived on schedule. The Home Fleet Admiral Tovey joined with the Wichita's Officers on the stern of the ship. Winston Churchill coming to the same meeting place visited with the crew. In the departure ceremony Ensign Talman was seated next to Mr. Churchill and shared his hymnbook with him as they sang hymns together.

With the *USS Wichita*'s departing from the Scotland Harbor and entering into the North Sea, Captain Low, who skipper of the ship, read the newest dispatch over the loud speaker system. The announcement advised the crew that the *USS Wichita* had been detached from the UK Home Fleet and that they were en route to the United States.

Ensign Talman at Casablanca

On October 24th 1942 the *USS Wichita* was en route to Casco Bay, Maine to join with a Task Unit that included another Cruiser, a Battleship, and many screening Destroyers. This Task Unit would be joined with two other Task Units departing from Hampton Roads, Virginia and Charleston, South Carolina. All were proceeding south and west toward the west coast of Africa.

Winston Churchill had prevailed on President Roosevelt that the "first priority" should be "Europe First." This was part of the plan. The Wichita recently released from the assignment with the British Home Fleet would be a leader in the conquest against the Nazi Forces. The Task Force's purpose was to place troops on western African shores of (1) Casablanca, in (2) Dakar in Senegal and (3) on the shores of Algeria in the Mediterranean Sea.

It was not known whether the Vichy French Forces would fight for Germany or remain neutral. The Wichita Task Unit was assigned to the Casablanca operation and it appeared the Vichy Forces were not prepared. Each ship's Captain of the Vichy Fleet in Casablanca Harbor was left to make his own decision. The Vichy Fleet was composed of Battleships, Cruisers, Destroyers and Submarines.

The *USS Wichita* upon arrival in the harbor commenced to fire on the ships in the harbor. The Vichy French Battleship, (*Jean Bart*), though tied to the dock returned fire. The Vichy French Cruiser, named *Primauget,* had cleared the harbor and brought the *USS Wichita* under fire killing 14 American sailors before she was silenced. Shifting targets the *USS Wichita* brought the Vichy French Destroyers under accurate fire. Meanwhile the Vichy French Submarines were trying to leave the harbor as they dispatched their torpedoes. The *USS Wichita* successfully out maneuvered three of the hastily dispatched torpedoes while the fourth was set too low and passed beneath the hull of the *Wichita*. By 2:00 p.m. the harbor resistance was fully diminished but the Wichita continued to destroy designated land targets.

Three days later on 12 November 1942 with the beaches secured, the *USS Wichita* received a report of the Naval Battles at Guadalcanal and the Coral Sea. The Japanese had sunk two heavy Cruisers, one American and one Australian, plus two light American Cruisers on November 8, 1942. This left the Pacific Fleet in need of Cruiser firepower. (The reader must remember the loss of Battleships in Pearl Harbor). The *USS Wichita* was detached from the Casablanca operation and ordered to the New York Navy Yard for quick repairs from the damages caused by the Vichy French.

After a short Ship Yard availability the *USS Wichita* was en route to the Norfolk Navy Yard to replenish, re-arm and departed Norfolk December 6, 1942. With a quick transit through the Panama Canal the *USS Wichita* was in the Pacific Ocean and en route to New Caledona (Noumea) in the Hebrides Islands to strengthen Admiral Halsey's Fleet. On January 4, 1943 the *USS Wichita* reported for duty at their Fleet Headquarters at Noumea, New Caledonia, South Pacific.

The Diary

Ed Black, a US Navy veteran from North Carolina, had purchased and read my book *We Were There* which has to do with the rescue of the survivors from the *USS Indianapolis*. Ed dropped me a letter explaining, he too was a survivor. The story following is a combination of his letter and other material needed to round out the story.

Dear Peter:

Since I was also a survivor from WWII I thought you would like to hear the story of *My Diary*. With Ed Black's letter was a copy of a news report by Dennis Rogers in the *News and Observer* of Raleigh, NC dated 06/18/1987. I also have a report on the *USS Rich* from the Tin Can Sailor quarterly newspaper dated June 2003. A quick summary of Operation Overlord follows and then Ed Black's diary comes into play telling a most unusual story.

Operation Overlord, scheduled for June 6, 1944, was the planned invasion of the Normandy shores of France. The Naval part of the invasion was named "Operation Neptune." German Field Marshall Erwinn Rommel had intensive defense plans to prevent the Allied Forces from making a landing on Normandy.. He called the area a "zone of death" and had placed underwater barricades of steel, cement and other devices to puncture ships hulls when the ships passed over the "death zone." In addition there were four million mines just below the surface, awaiting any ship or craft that would approach the beach areas. On the shore overlooking the sea area was every conceivable gun emplacement known to the German High Command. Rommel believed if the mines and barricades didn't stop the amphibious assault, the withering firepower would.

The US fire-support ships included three Battleships, three Cruisers and thirty-nine Destroyers and Destroyer Escorts. The Destroyer type vessels besides bringing their guns to bear would escort the Battleships and Cruisers and search for enemy submarines. During the course of the landing the German firepower was intense as was the equally answering guns from the American Battleships, Cruisers and Destroyers. With a small break in the action Ed Black was able to make an entry in his diary.

Now a diary was a forbidden item during the war. In case you were captured it could reveal much information to the enemy. Ed was successful in keeping it from his Division Officer's eyes. Using his pencil he made the following entry in his diary.

"We are all thanking God that we went through the night without a mishap. During the time since the invasion has started we have only slept a few hours and have eaten very little food. All of us are nervous and jumpy. At the present time, the USS Nevada, the ship we are protecting, is shelling a town over on the coast with her large guns. If we come through this OK, we will be lucky. However our trust is in*God to see us through safely."

He wrote these few lines and then shoved his diary in his back pocket. These would be the last words written in his diary on June 8th 1944. Shortly after this Ed's ship, the *USS Rich* (DE 695), was summoned to rescue sailors in the water from a nearby sunken Destroyer. Rushing into an unswept mine field to render assistance the *USS Rich* took two underwater explosions from mines which broke the ship's keel in half. The explosion threw Ed up and on a overhanging metal container. His injuries were severe. His skull was fractured, his jaw broken, his leg broken and his body suffered numerous shrapnel wounds. He knew he must abandon the ship. Fortunately his good friend, Carlie

Black from Thomasville, NC. was there to see that they both got over the side and away from the sinking ship. They were able to get to a floating raft which held four others. Ed and his friend hung on awaiting help. It was here that Ed passed out. He was alive but unconcious for 31 days. Gradually he recovered, was granted leave and sent home to North Carolina. He never thought of his diary again. He was sure it was lost in the sea.

Time passes and on June 6th 1984, the 40th anniversary of the Invasion, Ed returned to the Normandy Beach. Standing on he beach, he searched the sea where the *USS Rich* was sunk. On the back of his jacket it read, "Ed Black, USS Rich." Suddenly someone call his name and he walked toward that person wondering who he was and why he called his name. He was Frank Calvo and from Connecticut. Calvo was filled with emotion and blurted out, *"I got you out of the water when the USS Rich sunk. I can't believe you are still alive. You were more dead than alive when I removed you from the water."* Ed studied his face and realized Calvo was very emotionally upset and appeared to be seeing a ghost. Ed asked for his address and told him he would contact him when he got back in the states. Time passes while Frank Calvo and Ed Black exchanged telephone calls and correspondence and they finally agree to a meeting in April 1985.

Ed went to Connecticut to meet Frank Calvo. They had dinner and then Calvo told Ed he would like to return something that belonged to him. With that he handed Ed his now 41 year old "diary." At this point Ed thought he was about to pass out, but he didn't. Ed said, "I welled up with emotion and tears filled my eyes." Frank Calvo said, "The diary fell out of your pocket when I cut your bloody water soaked clothes off." Calvo kept the diary all these years believing Ed had died. Calvo felt that there was no way Ed could still be living knowing his weakened condition. Here's what followed while Ed was semiconscious and being held up in the sea by his buddy Carlie Black.

Two Allied PT boats recovered the survivors and brought them to the LST 57 which provided the medical help sorely needed. Frank Calvo wrote the final entry in the diary that had fallen from Ed's back pocket. Frank wrote, *"It was a miracle that any of the survivors lived after being so badly blown up. We worked like mad taking care of them and the fellows appreciated it. Some of them weren't so lucky as four of the six passed away. We did all we could for them."* The rest of the pages in the diary are blank.

Ed reflecting on the meeting said, *"I never thought I would meet the man who saved my life so I could hug and thank him!"* Reflecting back over the 40 plus years since Ed's last entry in the diary he wrote this in his letter, *"It would take a real mathematician to figure the odds of our meeting. After 40 years, who would believe that two men would find each other on the same beach, on the same day because of the printing on the back of a jacket?"*

The diary written in pencil, stained by his blood and the waters of Normandy is now in the French Museum there in Normandy. This museum is dedicated to the men who came to Normandy to free the French from the Nazi scourge during WW II. Without the forbidden diary the rescued and rescuer would never have met personally and his story would not be in this book.

At the end of paragraph five * Ed Black said, *"Our trust in God will see us through!"* Ed was right, his God had seen him through.

Julian B. Jacobs' Captured Spy

Julian B. Jacobs of Richmond Virginia entered the US Army service in the middle of the year 1944 and was sent to train in an Army Traffic School in Michigan. Upon completion of his training he was shipped over seas to help direct and control the road traffic in the Franco-German area of Europe. But before you read this story you must have this background

At this time in December 1944, the "Battle of the Bulge" was ensuing. As the Allied forces approached to cross the Rhine River they found themselves facing a strong stand by the German Army in and around the Ardennes Forest. The Germans planned for a quick break through toward Antwerp and thereby cutting the Allied forces into two separate forces making them easier to defeat. Under a heavy fog cover, thirty-eight German divisions struck along a 50-mile front. The German mechanized Divisions over ran several of the American's First Army positions. Because of the "bulging shape" of the Ardennes Forest it was called the Battle of the Bulge. Brigadier General Anthony C. McAuliffe, leading the 101st Airborne Division, was surrounded and approached by a German Officer demanding his surrender. It was then that McAuliffe gave his famous answer, "Nuts!" This reply completely astounded the German Officer who reported the retort to his senior officer with the German word *NERTZE*. This left both officers with a quizzical look on their faces, not having ever heard the American slang used in such a manner.

Meanwhile the need to get reinforcements to the area is great, so General Bradley asked General Patton when he could get his troops, now in the South, back North to help the embattled Army in the Ardennes bulge. Patton replied, "He and his troops would be there within 48 hours!" At this point I can introduce Julian Jacobs.

Private First Class Julian Jacobs, fresh from traffic school is now directing any and all traffic heading South, to turn around and head back North toward the Ardennes Forest to help the beleaguered forces. Also at this time all officers driving Jeeps and Command Cars have been directed to cover the stars painted on the cowls of their vehicles. The cowl is the metal just under the vehicles windshield. The stars indicated these were Officer vehicles and German snipers were picking off the Officers. A canvas cover was provided to cover the stars.

Julian Jacobs, US Army stops enemy spy vehicle.

Well, down the road, heading south comes a Command Car showing three large white stars on the cowl. So traffic director, Jacobs pulls the Command Car over to see who this Officer is and why is he not obeying the rules. The driver, who is alone in the Command Car answers Jacobs' questions in English but with a very definite German accent. Well, that is all the Jacobs needs to hear, as he brings his Thompson Sub Machine to bear on the driver and directs him to dismount the vehicle. When queried again as to who he is, the driver states he cannot tell him. Well Jacobs just knows he has captured a spy and he has a "Silver Star" in the making. Queried again, the driver refuses to tell him who he is, but states if he can make a telephone call from the guard house he will bring someone who will answer his questions. Jacobs, poking his gun muzzle in the driver's ribs, guides the German accent-speaking driver to the guardhouse. A telephone call is made and in the next ten minutes there is a flurry of US Army Jeeps, Command Cars and regular Sedans with ranking Army personnel unloading from their vehicles. Surely with this display of rank and activity his "Silver Star" is a shoe in. Yes indeed, Julian Jacobs has caught a "Spy, of note."

The American Officers arriving chat back and forth shaking hands and greeting the driver in a quiet but warm manner and then one speaks saying, "Okay, Let's go!" "Well, wait just a minute here!" says Jacobs. "This is my prisoner and he is not going anywhere as long as I have this loaded Thompson at the ready!" The senior Officer steps forward speaking to Jacobs saying, "Son, you are doing a good job, but your prisoner is on our side and happens to be Prince Bernhard of the Netherlands." Reluctantly Jacob yields to the Senior officer's directions as the Prince walks to his command car. Jacobs calls out, "Tell him to cover those stars on the cowl before he gets killed!"

The War in Europe ends and Jacobs returns to Richmond where he tells family and friends about how he almost was awarded a "Silver Star" for catching a spy who turned out to be a Prince. Each time he tells it there is a little more embellishment added. Then one day his hand is called.

His 13-year-old daughter has been picked to be an exchange student through her school activity. She will be exchanged with a student living in the Frisian Island area of the Netherlands. Julian's wife jokingly suggests that since he met a Prince during the war why doesn't he write his "Prince" in the Netherlands indicating his daughter will be in the Netherlands on an exchange program. Quietly from his office Jacobs writes the Prince reminding him of their meeting during the war.

In a very short time a letter arrives at Jacobs' residence. Jacobs' wife is excited and reports that the letter carries a "gold seal" on the back of it. She encourages Jacobs to hurry home and open it, for she is dying to learn its contents. The opened letter is from the Prince Bernhard and it reads to the effect, *"I remember well our meeting and will you please advise me where and when your daughter will be staying in the Netherlands?"* Jacobs by letter thanks him for his letter and advises the Prince when and where his daughter will be staying for the two weeks in his country.

The exchange student plan goes as scheduled and Jacob's daughter is housed in the Netherlands school dormitory with her classmates. As a student she finds things all proceeding nicely then one day she glances out her dormitory window to see a large group of people following the mailman to her dormitory. It seems the mailman recognized that the special letter was from the Prince Bernhard and for a dormitory student. He told some of the townspeople about the letter he was about to deliver. Well, that did it! The word got spread amongst the local citizens and curiosity motivated them to follow the mailman on the day he was about to deliver this "Princely Letter." Not only did the mailman deliver the letter, but he called her from inside the residence and asked, that if she would, please read the letter aloud for all to hear its contents.

The letter was an invitation requesting the 13-year-old daughter to have tea with Prince Bernhard and his mother Queen Julianna at a set date and time. Further the Prince would send his automobile to pick her up and would also return her to her dormitory.

Well, the 13 year old daughter graciously accepted that tea and has since then enjoyed several more teas because Julian Jacobs family all have been invited to meet the Queen and enjoy a Royal Tea in the Netherlands.

The most recent Royal Tea occurred when Julian Jacobs' granddaughter accompanied by her mother enjoyed a Royal Tea in the Netherlands. The mother of the grand daughter invited to the recent tea was the 13-year-old exchange student and the original invitee to have tea with the Royals of the Netherlands.

Mrs. Julian Jacobs, now a great grandmother, has been heard to say that when the soldiers and sailors come home with their stories, listen carefully because you might be receiving an invitation for a Royal Tea some day.

Source: Oral history told at a Richmond Council, US Navy League luncheon.

The Royal Tea

Three Landings – No Band-Aids
Robert A Stansbury GM 1c USNR

He was on an LCT(A) which is a Landing Craft with an "armored" hull carrying three Sherman Tanks. It was 6:30 a.m., known as the "H" hour and the amphibious wave is making the first approach to Omaha Beach, Normandy. The date is June 6th, 1944 and there are twenty-six LCTs in line making this attack. The sea is rough for a flat-bottomed boat. The sky has gray clouds hanging low in a foreboding cast as each craft wends it way to the French shore.

On the edge of the cliffs above Omaha Beach, the chatter of German machine guns is interrupted intermittently by the boom of the large German 88's higher on the cliffs of the beach. Over the landing party's heads is the hum and sizzle of the missiles fired by the American and British warships giving evidence of broadside gunfire in answer to the German salvos.

Automatically the Allied soldiers en route to the beach in the landing crafts tuck their heads into their shoulders in a gesture of self-preservation. Later those surviving soldiers rushing ashore will be known as the "band of brothers" for they will be baptized in the bloody salt water there on D-Day on Normandy beaches.

Stansbury's LCT #2037 is part of the 26 LCTs which are bringing the tanks and soldiers onto the beach. The tanks guns will answer the large German guns. The Allied troops are under intense firepower from the entrenched German forces and are scrambling from the surf to get under the protection of the sheltering cliffs. Here they regroup and will continue their mission of the invasion. This French Coast is now a German wall designed to prevent the Allied invasion. It must be penetrated if the Germans are to be defeated.

There are also "12 Frogmen" aboard Stansbury's LCT

#2037. The Frogmen are being equally dispersed from the port and starboard sides of his craft. Stansbury is helping a Frogman whose hometown is Colonial Heights, Va. This is just 20 miles south of Stansbury's hometown in Virginia. The Frogmen need assistance in strapping the explosive charges on their backs. These charges are used to blow up the barriers installed by the enemy to disable the landing craft. Once the area is cleared for the landing boats, Frogmen then place markers indicating safe passage to the beach. Stansbury offers to keep some of the Colonial Heights Frogman's personal gear until he returns to reclaim it. Unfortunately all the Frogmen were lost. When the war ended Robert Stansbury sought out and returned the personal gear of that Frogman into the hands of his parents still residing in Colonial Heights, Virginia.

Meanwhile the bullets and shells sound like hail and thunder as they bounce off and echo on the steel armor protection of the LCT(A). Once the three Sherman tanks and frogmen are discharged from his LCT(A) Stansbury withdraws from the beach and proceeds back to the flotilla for more equipment and troops for the next wave of the invasion. At the moment of withdrawal from the beach, the Lieutenant who is Boat Officer of Stansbury's LCT(A) is wounded. Stansbury renders temporary medical aid and now heads to the sea borne battleship *USS Arkansas* for medical help for the Lieutenant. With medical aid received, the Lieutenant orders his landing craft to a large Liberty ship now at anchor and out of range from the German shore guns.

From the Liberty ship they load the soldiers with their equipment and then they are off again racing for the beach. The Lieutenant is unaware of the many punctures his LCT(A) has received above the water line of his craft. When empty of the tanks and frogmen the craft rode high on the surf when he proceeded to the Liberty ship. Now fully loaded with men and their equipment the craft sits lower in the water as they head to the beach. The punctures in its hull give evidence of their presence and soon leaks are springing from the many holes in its sides. Even though the craft was rated as armored, its water-tight integrity has been punctured. A call for assistance is given and a nearby LST (Landing Ship Tank) comes to rescue the men from the sinking craft. The equipment is lost with Stansbury's LCT# 2037. Stansbury and his LCT# 2037 shipmates are taken aboard and remained aboard the LST for about two weeks. Finally Stansbury and his surviving shipmates find passage to England and are placed in a survivors camp awaiting transferred back to the States. Stansbury received a 21-day leave, but a trained Gunners Mate just doesn't sit idle in the States in wartime. His orders to a new ship were announced when he received his leave.

He is treated to a six-day train ride across the States and is en route to Camp Elliott, California. Here he reports for a brief retraining session and then goes aboard his new assigned ship, the LSM #49. A brief explanation is needed here. The letters for example—L means landing, S means a commissioned Ship and the M, means motorized units are carried. Sailing out of San Diego, it is a quick trip to Pearl Harbor to refuel and replenish plus picking up the Marines who were waiting transportation to the war front. The next port of call is Agana Harbor in Guam where refueling and replenishment occurs again in the westward advance.

Now comes a new word to Stansbury's vocabulary. The new word is **Iwo Jima**. This is a small volcanic island located 700 plus miles south of Japan. This island is needed as an emergency landing or air launching base for American aircraft and is about half way between Guam and Tokyo, Japan.

There is one thing Robert Stansbury, Gunnersmate 1/c knows, and that is the LSM, like all amphibious crafts, is designed for landing on beaches. He has had his first beach strike experience at Normandy and now he is scheduled for a second one on Iwo Jima. If this were a baseball game two strikes is not the best position in a batter's box. In his first batter's box there never were any soft incoming as he recalled. That incoming bounced off the hull of his last ship and was the cause of his LCT(A) sinking. Well duty calls and Stansbury is in the wave of amphibious ships steaming toward the sands of Iwo Jima. The firepower was horrific as the Japanese were dug in and had a mean crossfire on the invading troops. The LSM #49 received some hits from Japanese guns but none of his crewmates were hurt except for some burns caused by phosphorus shells. He watched a flag raised on Mt Suribachi. Then he saw a second larger and more visible flag raised again by the Marines. He knew it would be a sight that would never be forgotten. When the Island was finally declared secured his LSM #49 was ordered back to the States for repairs.

The 30-day leave sat well with him but better still was the fact that he had come through another tremendous battle without a scratch. He knew he would be ordered back into the fray and he prayed his luck would continue. The amphibious forces were now in the thick of battles. He knew his experiences and skill would put him back on the front line.

His leave ended and upon reporting back to his ship he learned that he would be entertaining a close look at the beaches of Okinawa. So far he survived two invasions. Stansbury found himself still in that batter's box contemplating his third strike on foreign shores. Again a horrendous battle, and this time his ship was really harassed by the kamikaze pilots whose aircraft were flown so low over the water he could see the Japanese pilots faces. His ship was between the picket line and the main combatant forces. The picket line is composed of a line of anti-aircraft destroyers, destroyer escorts and smaller craft representing a line of defense for the major war vessels doing the heavy bombardment to soften the shore batteries before the landing takes place. The picket line is to prevent the enemy aircraft from crossing their line of defense from attacking the Battleships, Carriers and Cruisers engaged in the shore bombardment.

With the capture of Okinawa and Iwo Jima and the bombing of Hiroshima and Nagasaki the Japanese surrendered (August 14, 1945). Stansbury's LSM was directed to assist in the occupational landings in Japan. On September 21, 1945 with many troops aboard his LSM #49 they are in company with many other amphibious craft en route to Wakayama, Japan. The narrator of this book was aboard one of the escorting ships, namely the USS *Bassett* (APD 73) which helped guide the Task Force to Wakayama, Japan.

Here again American soldiers perform another invasion but this time with a peaceful walk ashore. After three walks ashore under horrendous conditions, the fourth walk was an easy for Stansbury as it is in a baseball game. His participation in three landings, (Normandy, Iwo Jima and Okinawa) gave him enough points for the "Magic Carpet." This was his oneway ticket back to the States. In December 1945 he received his honorable discharge and a railway ticket to his home in Richmond, VA.

In summary Stansbury had participated in the three historic landings. He had sailed the Atlantic and Pacific Oceans, saw Pearl Harbor and the USS *Arizona* on the bottom there. He witnessed both of the flags raised on Mt Suribachi. He had a ship sunk from under him, but kept his feet dry thereafter. He left his footprints on the shores of Japan. All this he did and never called for as much as a "band-aid." As a veteran of the three bloodiest invasions of foreign lands of World War Two, he is qualified for a membership in the "band of brothers." Well-done, faithful Gunners Mate First class, Robert Stansbury.

Source: Oral History & Memoirs recorded by his loving wife Frances Stansbury.
Note: The lines following were in the papers from Stansbury.

Ode to the LCT

Here's to the men who sail the seas
On the bucking decks of the LCTs.
The Battleships, Cruisers and Destroyers as well
Get all the glory, while the LCTs catch hell.
And when it's all over and the work is done
And the medals are given to the men who won,
And outfits are lauded by the powers that be,
Forgotten as usual, are the men of the LCTs

Composed by
Lt (jg) James W. Howard
USNR of Richmond. VA.

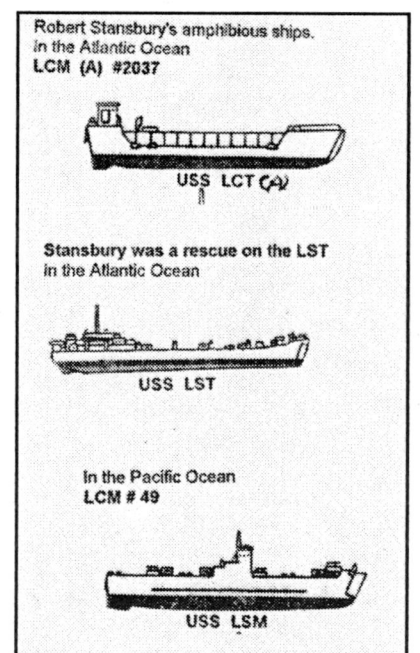

Robert Stansbury's amphibious ships.
In the Atlantic Ocean
LCM (A) #2037

USS LCT (A)

Stansbury was a rescue on the LST
in the Atlantic Ocean

USS LST

In the Pacific Ocean
LCM # 49

USS LSM

Chapter Three
(From Singapore to Tokyo)
(Prisoners of War Introduced)

An Overview – Pacific

Parade of Events – Pacific Area

POW James Manley, British Naval Officer
Bridge Over River Kwai

POW Lieutenant Alma Kent, QAANS
Singapore – Chanji Prison
A Christmas Letter

POW Colonel Wm. A. Lee, Gunney, USMC a.k.a.
Ironman Lee

POW William I Bragg US Army
Bataan-Corregidor Death March
Palawan Massacre and Formosa Prison Camp

POW Mario Tonelli, US Army
The Return of the Ring

Lt. General Wainwright's Letter
Corregidor's Surrender May 5, 1942

Tokyo Rose – American Citizen
Also a POW Being Held in Tokyo, Japan

Note: After you have read these stories, please remember it took the Atomic Bombs to end the war and to free these Prisoners of War once we learned where imprisoned.

An Overview – Pacific

With the completion of Robert Stansbury's Normandy story the reader has moved from the Atlantic Theater to the Pacific Theater. This chapter will carry you into patriot's stories in the Pacific. The Parade of Events early in this chapter will help the reader follow the calendar of time as Japan moved steadily through Manchuria and China. With the fall of France to Germany in June 1940, Japan moved south into French Indo-China and was threatening Burma-Indo lands and the Gibraltar of the East— Singapore. The reader has already learned of Churchill's and Roosevelt's North Atlantic secret meeting and the transfer of British troops to this area who are now captured.

Further the Pacific Ocean is such a wide expanse of sea that there is a great need to establish American Air bases on unsinkable islands from which the war can be fought. The Japanese controlled many Island groups, such as the Carolines, the Marshall, the Gilberts and the Marianas. Lacking Island bases, and with the Battleships sunk in Pearl Harbor, the American Carriers had to carry on the war effort until we could rearm again with a Naval Battle Force. Both the Japanese and American Navies were in transition as the Carrier with its multiple flights of aircraft could carry the battle to the enemy before the enemy's Battleships were in firing range. The attack on Pearl Harbor brought home the lesson of aircraft carriers. The Japanese Fleet launched its plane 275 miles from Pearl Harbor. The aircraft did their damage and returned to their carriers and sped away to Japan before we got ammunition boxes unlocked. They were kept locked because of the fear of saboteurs on the bases in Pearl Harbor.

The Battleships and Cruisers in the past had to fight a war within visual sight of the enemy ships and had to be successful in placing mortal shots on the enemy's ships. Cruisers, in the earlier days, carried a "scouting airplane" which could search for the enemy over the limited horizon of a Battleship. When the electronic device called "Radar" was introduced the radio beam's echoes could tell the enemy's location as well as his course and speed. At this time in Naval Warfare the Aircraft Carrier was now the formidable force that could engage the distant enemy with several air attacks, return to the carrier to refuel, to rearm and again be launched to continue the attack.

Fortunately for the United States the Japanese command failed to demolish the fuel storage tanks located in Pearl Harbor. Fortunately also was the fact that the American Carriers were not in the harbor when the Japanese attacked. Though our large gun ships were briefly silenced, our air wing of trained pilots, and aircraft were still available to pursue the enemy.

This chapter starts the advance toward Tokyo from the recollections of captured men who waged this war. The reader will learn of a British POW captured near Singapore forced into slave labor. The reader will learn how noncombatant medical people are sent bathing to be shot in the surf and how a gutsy British Nurse protects her female charges but still loses one to the sword.

The inhumane treatment by a nation that once was a Geneva Convention member is beyond all human understanding. This brutality must be told so that all Nations will rise in chorus against such dastardly inhumane treatment in the future. The reader will also meet with American POWs of the Philippines, Peiping, China and coalmines in Japan. Patriots from different South Pacific Islands recite their stories, many of which have never reached history books, but are told here. The first story is of James Manley a rescued British sailor from the HMS Repulse, who endured as a

Prisoner of War helping to build the bridge over the River Kwai.

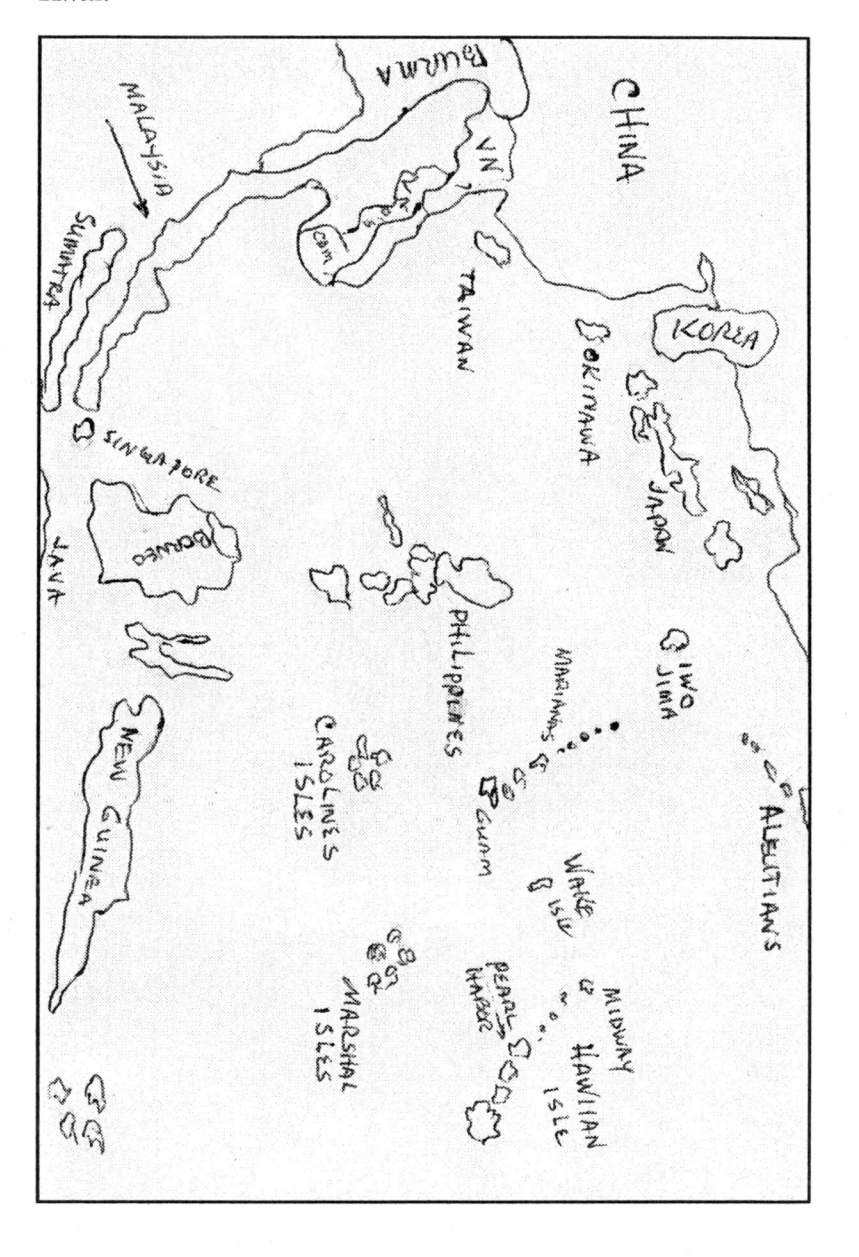

WW II Parade of Events — Pacific

Sept. 18, 1931	Japan invades Manchuria.
July 07, 1937	Japan invades China.
Dec. 12, 1937	*USS Panay* sunk in the Yangtze River. Japan apologizes even though the *Panay* was well marked as a USA Ship, 24 killed, 43 wounded.
July 24, 1941	Japan invades Indo-China
July 30, 1941	*USS Tutila,* (AO 44) attack on Yangtze River by Japanese Air Force. Japan apologizes.
Nov. 26, 1941	Secretary Hull hands counter offer to Japan regarding Indo-China and China which is rejected. Another proposal offered by Japan.
Dec. 05 1941	Japanese fleet of Carriers, Battleships, Cruisers depart Kurile Islands toward Pearl Harbor. Unless the recent offer is accepted Japanese fleet is to strike Pearl Harbor.
Dec. 07, 1941	Pearl Harbor is attacked at 0730 Pacific Time. Roosevelt declares war at 0100 pm EST.
Dec. 08, 1941	*USS Wake,* a gunboat surrenders to the Japanese after an attempt to scuttle the ship failed. This is the only American ship to strike her flag in World War II
Dec. 10, 1941	Off the coast of Malaysia the British *HMS Prince of Wales, HMS Repulse* and *USS Houston* are sunk. Singapore under siege. (85000 men British and Indian troops surrender to become POWs. Introducing James Manley & Alma Kent stories.)
Dec. 10, 1941	Japanese occupy Guam.

Dec. 10, 1941 Japanese land on Luzon Island, Philippines.

Dec. 10, 1941 US Marine detachment in Peking and Tientsin, China are taken as Prisoners of War. There are over 500 men captured. (Introducing Ironman Lee)

Dec. 11, 1941 Germany and Italy declare war on USA.

Source: World Book, 1968
American Naval History, Jack Sweetman, 1991

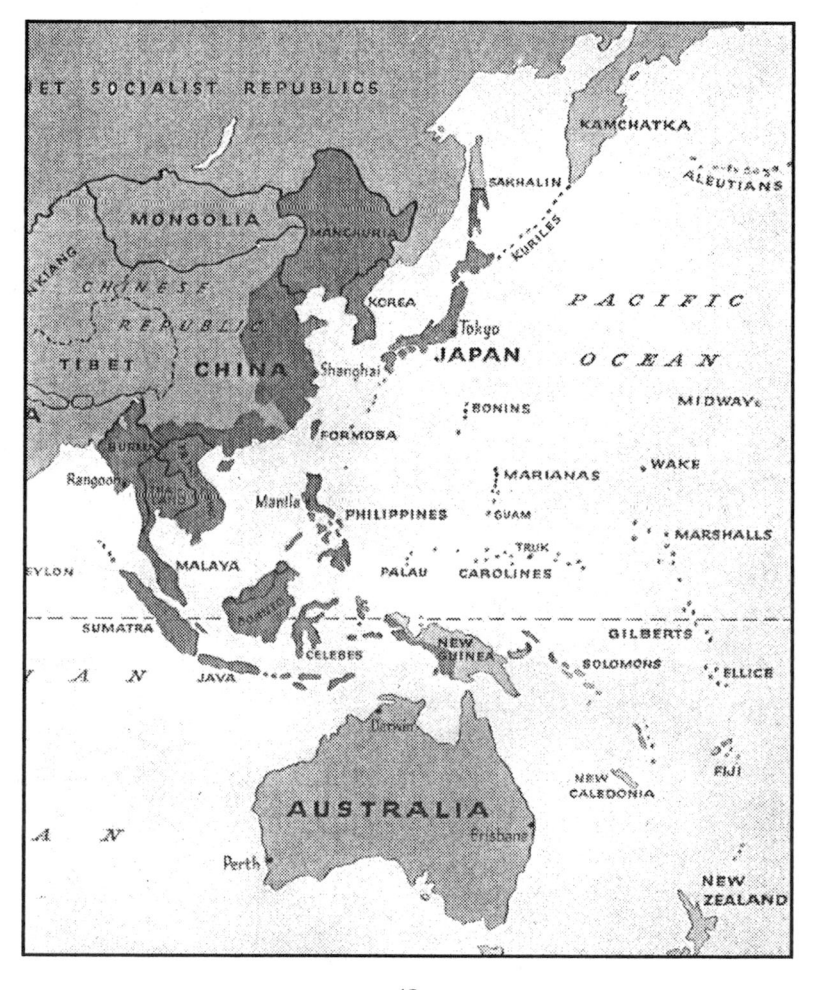

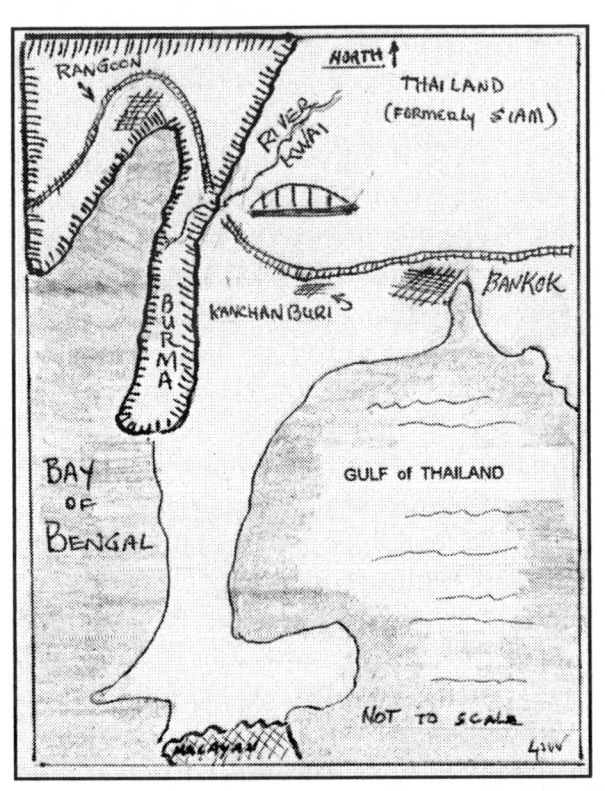

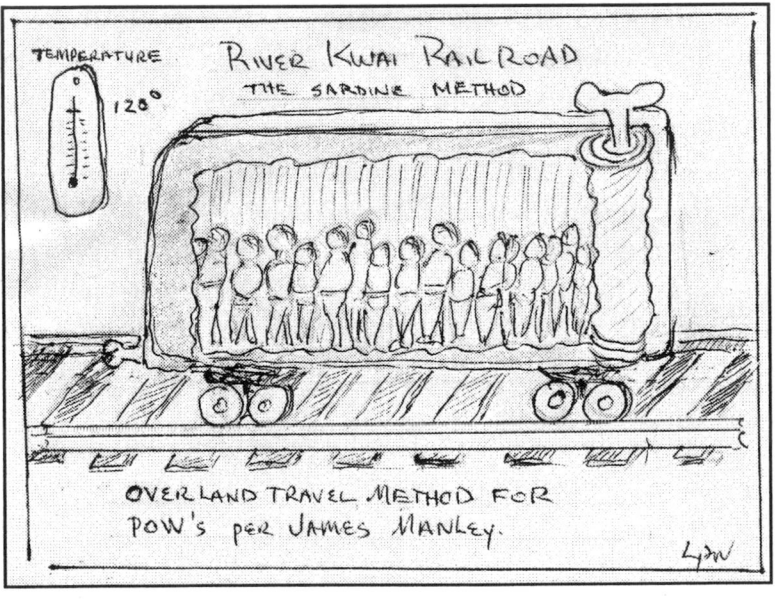

James E. Manley, POW
Bridge Over River Kwai

James' memoirs start with this statement.
"I was a young man when taken as a prisoner of war in December 1941. When released four and one half years later I was a repellently diseased old man." James Manley was a survivor of a wicked, political sacrifice dealt out by the barbarian nation of Japan. During his captivity he had imagined and convinced himself that his mission was to emerge alive from the various camps, the jungle and finally prison. The odds were against him and the tropical climate alone was capable of rotting anything including men."

James Manley had been a ship's Officer on the British ship *HMS Repulse*, which was sunk by the Japanese air bombers just off the harbor of Singapore. He was rescued by a Japanese vessel which was sunk shortly after and he was rescued again by the Japanese. Captured now and a prisoner of war (POW) he quickly learned that he and other survivors, were not to be recognized under the Geneva Convention rules for POWs. The treatment of POWs was established by the well-meaning nations participating in the League of Nations dogma. Japan had withdrawn from the League prior to her invasion into China. The typical Japanese military philosophy allowed no alternative to an enemy's surrender or captivity but death. POW's were dishonored, despised and the lowest form of human excrement. The Japanese military code held, "One who has been captured in battle is to be beheaded or castrated at the will of the Emperor" Fortunately, Manley slid under the Japanese code as he was not a "warrior in battle" but a survivor from a sinking vessel and therefore not beheaded nor castrated. The Emperor had other plans for such as these survivors.

In June 1942 the Emperor wanted the railroad completed to Bangkok in Burma and with the British and Chinese forces captured they had the slave labor force needed to achieve this goal. Manley explained that in an ordinary can of sardines there are 8 sardines in the can. Using that as an illustration Manley states that in a steel railcar pulled by a engine, 30 men were packed into this steel box eight foot wide and eighteen foot long and thus compacted they traveled north for 11 days in the tropical sun to the next rail junction named Banpong. The undulation of the rolling cargo railcar, with half sleeping and half waking motion, became hypnotic and dreamlike. It was the only way to survive. Was it 11 days or 11 thousand days when they arrived in Banpong?

Until now this bridge and railway had been considered impossible to build. In Manley's eyes this was equal to building a pyramid with bare hands through a jungle and in the most hostile terrain in the world. Further the railroad was to be completed in six months. With the forced labor driven to extremes, it was completed in October 1943. "If the men who died building were laid side by side," wrote Manley, "they would have roughly covered the 273 miles of the track."

Banpong was a junction point connecting the rail lines East and south Siam (now Thailand). Upon arriving in Banpong the POWs were housed in the low land leading to the swamps at the edge of the village. It was an indescribable clutter of filth, open drains, rats, rubbish, scurvy dogs and every conceivable variation of foul fly. For beds we lay on bamboo platforms just high enough to keep us out of the sewage that dribbled and eked to the low swamps. There was nowhere to go. There were no guards. If we did escape and they didn't kill us, then the locals would return us to the Japanese.

In his memoirs so far Manley doesn't mention food or fresh water. Manley continues, "After one night on the bamboo platform we started marching toward the area where the railroad construction would start. We marched in alternate day and night stages and covered 160 kilometers."

The frequent rainstorms turned the road into a quagmire of calf-deep black slime. To this day, Manley wrote, "I can still recall the bizarre sucking noise made by the hundreds of feet being put down and pulled out of the mud."

A camp was established and labor on the railroad began. Each day at first light we lined up for our ration of rancid rice and then a roll call was conducted in Japanese. If there was an absentee in the roll call then someone would be thrashed with a bamboo stick. Believe me, being beaten with bamboo is like being beaten with an iron bar.

When we reached the bare rock just above the River Kwai we were put to work cutting into it with hammer and chisel until it was too dark to see. When the rock was level and clear then we would move up the rail track. Soon Tokyo issued orders that the work must be sped up. The Japanese command felt due to the increasing POW deaths, caused by cholera, this would delay laying the rails. As a result of these orders we are now on the parade grounds at the first break of light for roll call. At this early hour a signal was given and we faced the East, bowing five times as we chanted the Japanese soldier's prayer. This imperial message chanted in Japanese is long forgotten.

The hard labor, the long hours and the small ration of food tended to drive us out of our minds. Add to this, is the curse of the jungle, the insects that literally ate us alive. At night after work, tired as we were, we were kept awake by the swarming of bed bugs that wandered over our bodies biting and sucking our blood. Giant centipedes wriggled into our hair and stuck their million poisonous feet into our scalps, setting our heads afire.

Food was scarce even for our Jap guards. Woes betide to any snake that came within killing distance for it ended up in the cooking pot. The boa constrictors were the most delicious. The vision of a yelling band of starving prisoners chasing a twelve foot silver rainbow colored python is an image that has stayed with me. It sums up the lunacy of that world.

As days dragged on our ranks got thinner. Hundreds of men had died by now in every foul and unimaginable way, while we, the hapless survivors, prayed it would not be our turn next. Unfortunately "death" was the number that came up most often in this POW lottery. By June 1943 cholera had traveled 125 kilometers up the rail from Camp Nikki to our location. Cholera was unstoppable. Once contracted, one quickly shrank and died within 24 hours. To reduce the source of the infection no more burials were performed. From then on our nights were illuminated not only from the burning fires in the center of the camp, but also by the glow of the funeral pyres that were sending all too many of our fellow POWs up in smoke.

Towards the end of October 1943 the rail track was completed and the ceremonial gold spike was driven into place. What lay ahead for the surviving POWs was yet to be revealed. It has been estimated that over 200,000 Allied prisoners and Asian laborers died to achieve this railroad that has since been swallowed by the jungle. The cholera-ridden jungle and the River Kwai valley are now fertilized by the remains of our friends who died building this folly.

Continuing Manley's memoirs are two items.

The first is: "On to Tokyo?" followed by the year 1944. Somewhere between the rail line completion in October 1943 and 1944 in Manley's notes he was able to catch and cook a cat. Catch and cook a guard dog, with curry spice, and catch and cook a rat. He added "gently fried they tasted like rabbit." These words probably shock the reader but you must remember the Japanese regarded the POWs as the lowest form of human excrement. Thank God he lived to tell the story. Let every generation read and never forget what these brave men suffered so that we might have a world rid of such despots and such a culture.

The second item is the one line. "American torpedo–Sumatra?" As best I understand it the Japanese ship on which Jim Manley was being moved to a new labor camp was torpedoed by an Allied submarine off the coast of Sumatra. Manley survived this sinking. He was recaptured by the Japanese and was again en route to another slave labor camp in Japan. (See George Clark's letter page 176.)

Manley indicated that he and many other POWs were stowed in the cargo hold space on a merchant Japanese ship. There was no food, nor water except everyday the Japanese crew would dump some watery slop to the POWs through the deck openings. He said the men were catching flies that were rampant in the hold area and eating them. There were no rest room facilities. They stood in their excrement.

James Manley was repatriated to Australia when the war ended and received sorely needed medical help with other military men there in Australian Rest Camps, who had not faced the isolation and incomputable experiences, his group endured. They felt that they were one step ahead in recovery over those who never made the trip to River Kwai. River Kwai survivors had a good grasp of the thorny stick of measurement to place against things that did or did not matter in life.

Even though the Japanese deliberately broke his right hand, ending dream of being a surgeon, he did not dwell on it. He accepted it as a part of his life and grew from it. He was never bitter about his River Kwai experience. After his release from British service he settled in New Jersey employed by a medical firm. Later he was transferred to Richmond, Va. but never sought American citizenship, remaining loyal to the "Crown."

He was a lay reader at St Bridget's Church, Richmond, Virginia and with his fine English speaking voice, it was a pleasure to hear him deliver the readings. I had always planned to visit with him on some of the details but death came before we could meet. James Manley died in September 16, 1994 and the requiem mass was offered by his priestly brother, the Reverend T. Francis Manley from Manchester, England. The church was full and there was not a dry eye in the pews of St Bridget's Church.

Source: Memoirs received from James Manley's gracious wife Martha Manley
Oral History when as a speaker at a Navy League Luncheon, Richmond, Virginia.

Addendum:

(1.) Many of the Americans who died building the bridge over the River Kwai were from the USS *Houston* sunk off Indonesia, December '41. (Source: *Richmond Times-Dispatch* 09/16/1997)

(2.) The Brits who survived from the Japanese War Camps are demanding compensation for their work. The Japanese Government in 1998 offered to pay for the British Prisoner's of War grandchildren the cost of one-year study in Japan as well as finance veterans visits to the battlefields and cemeteries. Brit's answer was, "We want proper compensation and not joy trips for 80 year old men to Japan." (Source: *New York Times*, 01-13-1998)

(3.) Quote: Sid Tavender, 75 who survived the Burma-Thailand railway. "We want nothing less than a full apology and compensation from the Japanese Government. We have been telling Mitsubishi for years to put one penny on the price of their cars to pay us back, but they never respond. " Each victim is seeking up to 10,000 pounds compensation. (Source: *The Sunday Telegraph*, London 09-19-1993) (See Alma Kent's Christmas letter to L. Peter Wren, next in this chapter)

POW Lieutenant Alma Kent, QAANS
Singapore – Chanji Prison
A Christmas Letter

It was in 1995 when my wife and I were visiting London and staying at the Union Jack Club on Sandall Street near Waterloo Station. Here we met several British Veterans from the Lost Fleet of the India, Burma Chinese Theater. The British sailors and their shipmates were enjoying a ship's reunion and they invited us to join them. This is when I met the remarkable Nurse Lieutenant Alma Kent, RN of the Queen Alexandra's Army Nursing Service. In the course of conversation with Alma Kent she recalled the suffering inflicted by the Japanese guards on the prisoners of war: Speaking out she said, " I was fortunate in that I lived through the war, but I watched many die, and I will never forget what the prisoners suffered as long as I live!" This is her story.

Alma Kent was born in Balleymena, Ireland on June 16, 1917 and the daughter of an Army veteran. After training as a nurse she joined the Queen Alexandra's Army Nursing Service and was stationed in Singapore. In February 1942 Singapore fell to the Japanese invaders and she was imprisoned in the infamous Chanji Prison. Chanji Prison is infamous because of the gross criminal, shocking and brutal treatment inflicted by the Japanese guards on the captured British, Indian, Chinese, Burmese and American (*USS Houston*) prisoners of war.

This experience occurs in Chanji, a city on the island of Singapore. Singapore is an island three quarters of a mile just south of the end of the Maylayan Peninsula. The city of Singapore is on the seaward tip of the same named island. Given now is the background prior to her story. Singapore fell to the Japanese Army on February 15, 1942.

(Sixty-eight days after Pearl Harbor) The Japanese military were brutal to all male captives. In addition to that they looked upon foreign women as their "Comfort Ladies" and targets to be violated. Lieutenant Alma Kent's duties involve the training of twelve female novices in the science of nursing. At age 25, how will Alma Kent protect her female charges? Before I answer that let's learn of the brutality other medical professional people endured from their captors at this time of World War II.

After all bed patients were slain, Medical staff were directed to go for a swim. All were machine gunned.

CASE ONE:

Shortly before the fall of Singapore a group of Australian Nurses made plans to transfer their wounded from the local hospital across the Malacca Straits to the Dutch Islands of Java and Sumatra before the Japanese invaders came. Unfortunately one of the boats transferring the wounded and their nurses sank near a small island called Banka. The nurses made their way ashore on the island and were eventually gathered together and directed by the Japanese command to go for a swim back into the surf. When the Nurses were about waist high in the surf the Japanese command ordered them machine gunned. All were lost in this barbarian act. The point to remember is that Medical people are not combatants and render medical help to all in need whether friend or foe. This brutal action by the Japanese is strictly forbidden by the Geneva Convention.

CASE TWO:

The Alexandra Hospital was the large Hospital on the Singapore Island and served medically for all the civilian, military and their dependents. When the Japanese captured the island, the Japanese soldiers commenced to kill everyone in the hospital including the staff, all doctors, all nurses, all patients and even those patients in surgical procedures. This is known as the Singapore Massacre. The point of this case is to remind the reader that Lieutenant Alma Kent and her twelve medical novices in training are now the only medical help left on Singapore Island. The question is how will the Japanese treat these females? These are not combatants but truly defenseless people. These Japanese soldiers are not fighting an armed enemy. There is no other way to say it. They are ruthless barbarians killing innocent defenseless people?

The Geneva Convention rules of 1929 applied to all nations. Japan had withdrawn from the "Rules of Conduct" which specifically stated doctors, nurses and medical aides are not combatants. Medical people do not carry weapons as do full time military personnel. Medical personnel may carry a gun in self-defense but never to kill or injure. Their dedicated work is to restore life and not to destroy it. In a war area they render medical service to both friend and foe and with equal compassion. What is going to happen to Alma Kent and her 12 female medical aides? Read on.

CASE THREE:

Nurse Kent rendered all the medical services she could after a Japanese guard who said a prisoner of war was too tall for him to speak with, so he cut his legs off to bring him down in size. These are terrible things to experience. So with firm resolve and at age 25, here is the action Alma Kent took in defense of her novice aides.

Lieutenant Kent presented herself to the Commanding Japanese Officer at Chanji. Speaking boldly with her British accent, she advises the Japanese Commandant that she and her 12 Medical Aides are the only medical help available. Being a noncombatant, she and her aides will render medical service to him and his troops as is necessary for their good health. In exchange for that service, he and his troops are not to molest or harm her or any of her young female personnel. After some considerate thought the Japanese Commandant agreed to abide by her requests in exchange for her medical help.

With no threat of becoming "Comfort Ladies" the regular camp routine took precedence in the days that followed. The morning sessions required everyone to gather on the drill field for roll call and hear the instructions for the day. At the completion of instructions and before dismissal, all present were required to bow their heads to the Camp Commandant. One of the medical novices, as observed by the Commandant, was not bowing her head at the dismissal. Lt Kent was called into the Commandant's Office and instructed that this certain novice was not showing respect by not bowing her head. Further, if she continued do so there would be consequences.

Lt. Kent informed the novice of what the Commandant wanted at the morning dismissal and that he will have his orders complied with. The novice, a bright and blue eyed young Irish girl, of whom Lt. Kent was fond, told Lt. Kent that she only bowed to her Lord and would not bow to the Commandant. The novice was as firm in her belief as the Commandant was in his order.

The next morning prior to dismissal the bow was called for and the novice's head remained upright where she stood. With that the Commandant ordered her tied up. That is to say, the guards put her in a prone position with her hands tied behind her back and her legs brought up to her buttocks and tied so she could not move. She was left on the drill field in that position in the hot tropical sun all day and in the sultry night that followed. There was no water ration provided nor a toilet break. There she lay in that position for 24 hours and until the next roll call. At the roll call she was untied and straightened up and left standing until it came time for the dismissal. When the bow was called for her head remained upright. With that the Commandant had her placed in a kneeling position and with his sword he beheaded her in front of all present. Lt. Alma Kent said the head rolled over to her foot and stopped there. Lt. Alma Kent says she will never forgive the Japanese for their brutality.

When the Japanese surrendered after the dropping of the atomic bombs in 1945 Lt Alma Kent was repatriated. Her weight was four stones English weight. Translated to American it is 4 times 14 or 56 pounds. She has her own reminders of the days while a prisoner of war. She wears metal plates in the back of her head and one in her leg. Alma makes her home in London and does voluntary work for charities. In particular she does a lot of volunteer work for the nuns of St Mary's of the Cross, which is a convent near her home. Alma is an avid "marathon runner" and began her running when she was 65 in 1982. She has run in over 199 marathons to raise money for charities and has lost count of the total funds she has raised. The largest sum she has won for charities occurred in 1992 when she completed the course in 3.5 hours and was awarded a gold medal.

In October 1998 (age 81) she had completed two one-half marathons in Chicago and planned to do another in New York City before Christmas. In a recent newspaper report when asked did she intend to keep running until age 100, she answered: "Hopefully longer than that.

(A copy of her most recent letter follows this story.)

Source: Alma Kent's oral History, letters from Bob McNichol of Canada,
World Book-Singapore, *Navy News*, dated Oct 1998, pg 30.

Lt. Alma Kent's Medical Aides answer roll call and told to bow to the Commandant. One Aide refused.

Alma Kent (BS-AN)
Queen Alexandra Australian Nurse Society

In December 2001 a Christmas card came from Alma Kent and it read as follows:

Dear Peter and Family:

I haven't forgotten you. Our last meeting was at the Union Jack Club where we all had tea, remember (10-05-95). (It was) Bob McNichol from Canada, Bill Clitherow & wife Bet and myself.

Well Peter, a lot has happened (to) all ones including myself who were P.O.W. s with the Japs. We all got 10,000 pounds. It is about time too. I am still running the marathons and I still cook for the nuns at the convent. I have been there now for 18 years. I am part of the furniture. I am now 84 years old but so fit I don't feel it. (Alma born June 16, 1917)

By the way I still have the drawing you done for me, remember?

(It is) a vase of flowers (which) you also signed it. You see I have kept it all these years. God Bless you Peter and may you have a very merry Xmas and a peaceful New Year 2002.

Love, Alma Kent
(BSA) QAANS

POW Colonel Wm. A. Lee, Gunney, USMC a.k.a.
Ironman Lee

The fact that Buck Private Wm A. Lee was born 12 November 1900 in Wardhill, Massachusetts, might lead you to suspect that there is a lot of the "1776 Minute Man's" patriotism in him. He enlisted in the Marine Corps in 1918 just before his 18th birthday in what then was called the "Horse Marines" and was shipped to France as World War One was winding down. During his tour of duty and because of his rifle marksman ability he was rated as a "Marine Gunner." Returning home from France in 1919 Lee was released from active duty but the love for the Marine Corps brought him back again to the Corps in 1921.

This young Marine increased his patriotism as he served under Captain Lewis B. "Chesty" Puller's command fighting the Nicaraguan Banditos. "Chesty" is so named because he is the most decorated Marine in Marine Corps history in addition to being a most outstanding leader of men.

Wm Lee's action was so outstanding against the Nicaraguan rebels that he was awarded three Navy Crosses. The Nicaraguan Bandito leader, Sandina offered a reward of $50,000 in gold to anyone who could bring Gunner Lee in dead or alive to the Bandito Commander. There were several heavy encounters with these Banditos. On one occasion, in a close fight, Gunner Wm Lee received a blow to his head which temporarily knocked him out. Gunner Lee remained unconscious for about 15 to 20 minutes as a result of the wound to his head. But when he recovered, he took over the Marine company's machine gun and used it with telling effect. He and his small group of Marines were 125 miles from their base and in a hostile jungle with enemy on all sides of them. Trapped two times by the enemy forces Gunner Lee routed the enemy with his accurate burst of firepower from the machine gun. A machine gun is usually operated from a three-legged tripod. The machine gun being operated during these skirmishes were from the strong arms and the two-legged stand of Gunner Wm Lee.

In Captain Puller's Action Report regarding Wm Lee's performance during these battling encounters he wrote the following,

"In the days of wooden ships and iron men, Lee would have been an iron man. Gunner Lee has been in twenty some engagements against the Banditos and while serving under me, he has distinguished himself by extraordinary heroism a number of times in the line of his profession. I recommend him for the Nicaraguan 'Crux de Valor.'" Thus Wm. A. Lee earned the nickname "**Ironman**" from one of America's most decorated Marines, Chesty Puller. The Nicaraguan "Crux de Valor" was awarded twice.

Lee after leaving Nicaragua participated in many rifle and pistol tournaments. He was a renowned marksman and out shot 5,800 competitors in the Wimbledon Cup Match. Twice he was on the Elliot Trophy team winners. In later years he was the instructor for the American Olympic Rifle teams teaching the art of shooting. So outstanding was Wm Lee's skill in firearms that in the 1990's the United States Marine Corps named the Quantico Marine Rifle Range in his honor.

In 1938 Lee was assigned to the US Embassy in Peking China. When Pearl Harbor was attacked on 7 December 1941 there was no way American Forces could extricate the Marine contingent assigned to protect the Embassy. Wm Lee and 204 Marines were so greatly outnumbered by the Japanese invading troops, that the US Officials ordered the Marines to surrender. On December 8, 1941, the Japanese Forces took over the Marine Camp at Chinwantao, which is just northeast of Tientsin, China. They transferred the Marines like cattle in ship's bottoms to the northern most island of Japan, named Hokkaido. The Officers were

penned up in a base on the side of a mountain. The enlisted were forced to work in the coalmines. Lee said, "We
were starved, beaten and tortured. My teeth were kicked
out because I protested to the treatment of American POWs.
My ears burned with cigarettes, and my hearing impaired
by blows to my head!" It was a brutal game the Japanese
soldiers played on the POWs. They stood the Marines at
attention and then commence to slap their faces and sides
of their heads until they got tired of it. If a POW fell during
these slapping sessions they stood him back up and continued the brutal punishment. The guards also found pleasure and amusement by placing a two by four upright on
the ground. The marines were then placed on their knees
with their chins supporting the upright two by four. Then
the guards would burn the Marines' ears with lit cigarettes.
If anyone flinched and the two by four dropped he was
taken out and was never seen again. Lee said he never
flinched. All these brutal acts occurred after a POW's full
day of working in the coalmines.

He was a prisoner of war for 44 months. He was a six-
foot man of 192 pounds when captured. When he came
out he was still six foot weighing 138 pounds. Any one who
fought back was immediately beheaded. All his finger nails
were pulled out During his torture he always lead the Japanese to believe he had another secret which he had not
revealed so he was left to live. They thought he would eventually weaken and tell them one day. He believed this tech-
nique kept him alive.

One day in August 1945 the Camp guards and people
were running around in panic and it appeared they were
very frightened. Lee said, "We had no way of knowing the
Atomic Bomb had been dropped on Japan, but the next
morning there wasn't a guard in sight. The following day
American planes flew over dropping food, clothing and
medicine in steel drums attached to parachutes. A few days

later the American Medical Corps arrived and told us the war was over. We were so burned out mentally and physically we weren't able to comprehend what had happened." The seriously ill were evacuated immediately. Those in a little stronger condition were given a few days rest with proper food and medication. When found strong enough to travel they were moved to the hospitals on Guam, in Honolulu or the American West Coast.

POW "IRON MAN LEE" suffered under Japanese imprisonment from January 1942 until August 1945. Here he is staked out for an "ear burning session" in which the prison guards put their cigarette butts out on the prisoners ears.

After brief stays in several Military Hospitals and Rest Camps, Ironman Lee returned to the States and ended up in Washington DC. He received orders to report to Quantico, Virginia. He called the Quantico Administration Offices reporting he was a Chief Marine Gunner and requesting transportation to Quantico. He was informed that there were no more rates called "Marine Gunner" and there was no transportation available for him. He had received no money because his pay records were lost when he was captured in China and nothing was done to bring his traveling papers up to date. Without proper papers the Navy Finance Officer could not disburse pay. So, without funds and in his weakened condition, he put his sea bag on his shoulder and walked the railroad tracks from Washington to Quantico to report under his orders.

At the Quantico Receiving Station he was asked for his personnel records. He told them the last time he saw them they were in the Finance Officer's files in China. Lacking the proper pay records to charge allowances off, the receiving Officer asked how did he get to Quantico. He told him he walked the railroad tracks until he got there. The finance Officer figured the taxicab fare from Washington, DC to Quantico and gave him chit for $14.80 which he then cashed for Lee. It had been 50 plus months since he had a payday.

Ironman Lee's only visible signs of injury while a Prisoner of War are , false teeth, damaged ears and a hearing aid. All of these items are a result of the brutal treatment he received from Japanese guards.. In spite of all that was meted out to him as a prisoner he continued to always have a positive uplifting attitude toward his fellowman and loved to talk with everyone about his beloved America, the American flag and his Marine Corps.

Ironman Lee died December 27, 1998 with a full Marine Corps internment service. In the company of many

Marine friends and his family, the narrator was there to pay honors to a true patriot. Below is what "Ironman" William Lee would recite at functions when he was asked to speak. The audience when "Ironman Lee" spoke would receive first hand the "Spirit of 1776." His presence would fill the room with a patriotism. As the reader continues to peruse these pages he to will feel Ironman Lee's patriotism. It lives on in the poetry he loved to recite and now is recorded in this book for all to know.

First: **A Veteran Speaks**

My hair has turned to silver
    And some of it has gone
My memory is fading
    And my teeth have lost their bite
I have an earphone and a pace maker
    And my frame, though worn, is still upright
And it is with pride I rise to stand
    Whenever I hear the music
Of a US Marine Corps Marching Band.

William A. "Ironman" Lee

Second: **Old Glory**

They named her "Old Glory,"
As she floats on the breeze
Which in legend, song and story,
As she waves over land and seas
Over ocean, lake and rolling river
And on the mountain glen or glade
With a fame that will live forever
There flies the banner that Betsy made.

Unknown

Third: **Our Flag**

When Freedom from her mountain height
Unfurled her standard to the air
She took the azure blue of the night
And placed the stars of glory there.
Together her crimson rays of light
Were joined with clouds of white
Alternating them with ease and grace
Until each stripe found its proper place.
Then from the mansion in the sun
She called her eagle bearer down
And placed the banner in his mighty hand
The symbols of our chosen land.
Our flag, Respect it, And protect it!

Unknown

Fourth: **The Last Tat-Too**

The muffled drums that roll their beat
    Sound the warrior's last tat-too
No more on life's parade will they meet
    The brave and fallen few
On fame's eternal camping ground
    Their silent tents are spread
And glory guards with solemn sound
    When the last tat-too is read
The price of freedom was blest
    By the fallen warriors now at rest.

Unknown

Source: Conversations with Colonel Lee and correspondence and various news clippings from Mrs. Ann Lee, widow of Wm. A. Lee.

POW William I Bragg US Army
Bataan-Corregidor Death March
Palawan Massacre and Formosa Prison Camp

William I. Bragg and I were friendly competitors work
ing for different automobile agencies in Richmond,
Virginia. Both of us had served four plus years in World
War Two. I had recently been released from the US Navy
after a two-year recall for the Korean conflict. Well, one
thing lead to another and soon I was telling him how my
ship, the *USS Bassett*, a fast transport ship, had placed US
Army troops ashore in the various Philippine Islands in
WWII to recapture the Islands from the Japanese. When I
mentioned the city of Puerto Princessa on Palawan Island,
I struck a nerve in Bill Bragg's memory. The following is
the story of a young Texan who was captured with the US
Army Forces on Corregidor Island which is located at the
mouth of Manila Bay. Here is Bill's story

Bill Bragg had enlisted in the US Army in September
1941. Upon completion of his basic training he was sent to
the Philippine Islands which at that time were "Protector-
ates" of the United States. He was rated as an infantryman,
forward observer (scout), and stationed on the Bataan Peninsula of Luzon Island. The Japanese attacked the Philippines on the 8th of December and began marching through
the many Islands. In the long and hard fight on the Bataan
Peninsula to slow the Japanese invasion, Bill was wounded
but not ready to surrender to the Japanese Forces. He decided he would swim to Corregidor so he could fight again.
The swim was a little longer than he realized and fortunately he was picked up by some Americans in a boat out in
Manila Bay.

Corregidor fought until they ran out of food, water,
ammunition and medical supplies. The only help

Corregidor received was that which an American submarine could bring. An American Submarine's ballast of guns
and ammunition were exchanged for the "Gold Bullion
Bars" and "Filipino Pesos" which were used to back the Filipino currency. Once the bullion was transferred, the submarine was en route to Pearl Harbor. The American and
Filipino forces surrendered on 6 May 1942. Now captured
the Americans and Filipino troops were marched to the
prison camps. It wasn't just one group but many groups
marching and estimated to be over 50,000 American and
Filipino captives in the Bataan Death March.

Baatan Death March May 1942. Rifle butt sport.

The roads were full of marchers who had to share the
same roads with the Japanese trucks. Often the truck drivers would swerve into the marching POW's killing and
maiming several of the POWs. If a POW was injured and
couldn't continue to march he was shot and his body kicked

off the road. Often other POWs would pick up the injured one and carry him in the continued march to prevent his early death. Also often the Japanese riding in the trucks would swing their rifle butts into the back of the POW's heads knocking them out or killing them with their blow. The Japanese riders would laugh heartily over the sport they were having.

They would not give the POWs any water but did allow them to fill their canteens with the contaminated water from the ruts in the road or from the caribou wallows, knowing it would eventually cause their death. Several times during the march Bill Bragg was beaten for what they considered delaying infractions. They would march POWs up to a well where they procured water for themselves but if a POW tried to get a drink they would bayonet him.

It took three days of marching to get to one of the two POW camps. Bill was at Cabantuan Camp which was considered the worst of the two camps. Later he was transferred to Billbid where he received less beatings for infractions or whims of the guards. Eventually he was moved to the Island of Palawan which separates the South China Sea from the Sulu Sea. With a group of 300 Americans of slave labor, they were to build an airfield. This was Bragg's home for two and one-half years. When the American Airplanes began to fly over the airfield on a regular basis, the Japanese felt the war was turning against them and that they should leave the area. There were not enough ships to move the 300 American laborers to the next site where they could continue to use this slave labor. Doing a one-two count off they divided the total POW labor force into two groups. Group two was marched into the air raid shelters they had dug into the side of a hill. Once the Japs had the full 150 men in the air raid shelter, the Japanese piled coconut logs on top sealing in the men. This was followed by dumping earth over the logs. When all logs were covered they poured gasoline on the pile and set it afire burning the trapped Americans alive. This is known today as the "PALAWAN MASSACRE"

In September 1944, Bill and balance of the 150 saved from Palawan Island were moved back to the Billbad Camp near Manila. About a month later about 500 POWs were put in the cargo hold of the hell ship "Sankyo Maru." There was hardly a place to stand because they were packed so tightly. The ship was destined for Formosa and it took 39 days as the ship sailed close to the China coast to avoid detection by American Forces.

Formosa (now called Taiwan) enjoys a hot steamy tropical sun as it straddles the Tropic of Cancer. In the cargo hold some men went crazy and would cry out only to be answered by the guards firing their guns down into the huddled mass in the hold. Feeding was done by lowering pails of slop into the horde of men who would fight for every crumb or morsel. They lived in their own urine and dung. Arriving in Formosa the POWs continued as slave labor in the lead and zinc mines. American airplanes bombed and strafed them daily not knowing they were American POWs.

Suddenly the bombing stopped. It was in August 1945. Bill didn't know the war was over until September 1945 when the Camp Commandant announced it to the POWs. The POWs had been planning to take over the camp. When the Commandant announced it, the POW leader gave the signal and the prisoners took over the guards of the camp. Later when the Allies discovered American POWs were on Formosa, they began to receive several air drops of food, clothing and medicine. Bill said unfortunately about 20 men who had survived the POW camps were killed when crates, being pushed out of an aircraft, landed on them.

As we talked that day, Bill laughed and said at one time he thought he was a goner! A crate landed near him and exploded and he thought he was covered with blood. He said to himself, " I have labored all this war to stay alive and then to be killed when the war is over by a damned air-drop!" He wiped his arm across this face and tasted the sweet taste of tomato juice. He said he went wild with delight. Bill went on further to tell of a fellow POW who constantly dreamed about the day he would be home. All he wanted was a big bowl of peaches. That would be the happiest home coming treat he could imagine. During the airdrop a crate landed near him and out rolled a #10 tin can. It was labeled "Peaches!" Bill said, "I believe the Lord listens to our prayers!"

To reinforce that last statement Bill went on to tell me about the gold ring his mother had given him before he entered the Army. Bill stated that his mother said she received it from her mother and she wanted him to have it. Bill said after he was captured he hid it in every crevice of his body so that the Japanese guards could not take it from him. He had learned that the Japanese guard was wary of anyone who was a religious freak. The guards would shy away from that person. Bill was able to make a little pouch in which he put the ring and wore the pouch around his neck. With a needle and thread he sewed a cross on the front of it. Whenever a guard asked or reached for the pouch he would announce in Japanese, "That's my Buddha!" With that announcement the guards would move away from him. He had learned some Japanese from a friendly young guard, and on occasions he would use their language to his advantage.

Speaking of "Buddhas," Bill said there were no atheist in the POW camps and that they prayed every day. Like all POWs, Bill suffered from malaria, beriberi and dysentery. He was wounded three times and later in life the Veterans Administration determined him to be 100% disabled.

William I Bragg has passed on to his reward but I have

saved these notes knowing someday I would set them down for the younger generations to read and learn what a gift of freedom they have received from Veterans of WWII. Further by our winning the War in 1945 we freed the Philippine people from the savagery and brutality of ruthless leaders. God Bless America! Let all nations know we come to restore human rights, to seek peace for all nations for we are our brothers keeper.

Source: My recollections and notes on Bill Bragg's POW experiences, *World Encyclopedia* and Richmond newspaper article by Dean Levi dated 04-09-'82

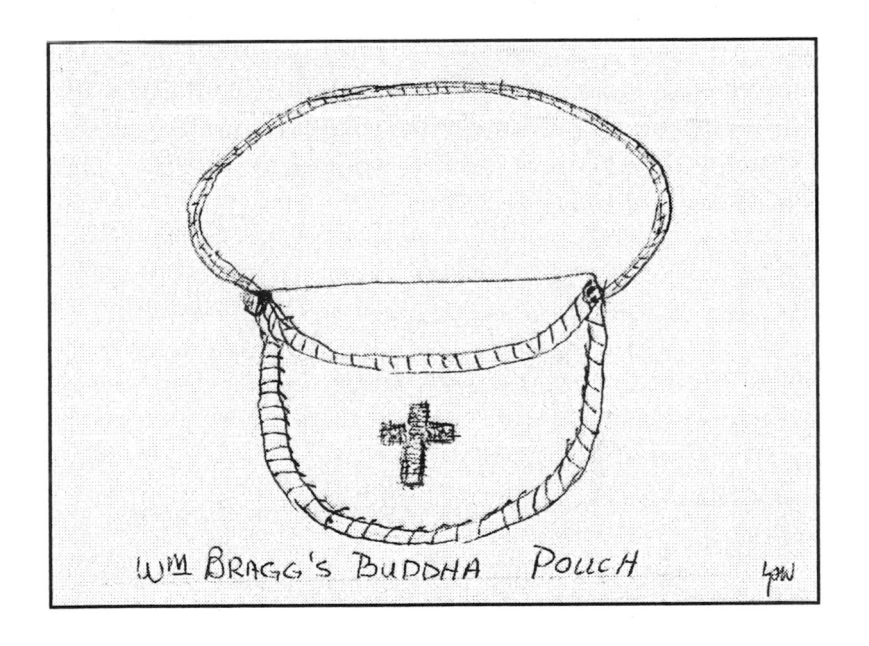

WM BRAGG'S BUDDHA POUCH

POW Mario Tonelli, US Army
Football Great – University of Notre Dame

In the previous story you learned about how a homemade Buddah pouch saved a mother's wedding ring from a demanding Japanese soldier. This story follows Bill Bragg's story because it is of a similar happening surrounding another treasured ring.

The Return of the Ring

Mario Tonelli, a Chicago lad, was a star football halfback for the Notre Dame team. In the game with the University of Southern California and prior to World War II, Mario made a spectacular long run for Notre Dame. He scored a late quarter touch down making Notre Dame the winner in a hard contested game. A gold ring was awarded to each Notre Dame player as a memento of the game. Mario treasured his ring,

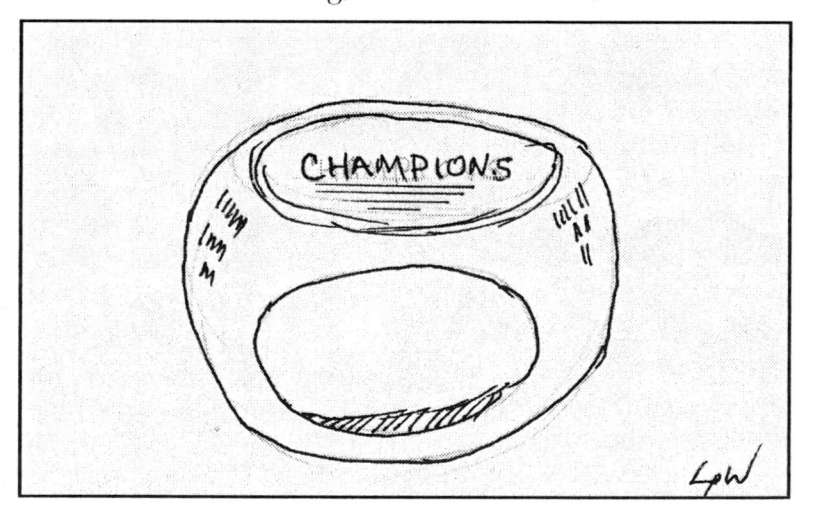

Mario Tonelli's Championship gold ring won in the football game when University of Notre Dame defeated the University Southern California.

Mario was captured in WW II by the Japanese and had the gold ring in his possession. A Japanese Guard seeing the ring wanted it and Mario would not give it up. His fellow American prisoners urged him to part with it or else he would part with his life. With reluctance he relinquished the ring. A few days later he was confronted by a Japanese Officer who wanted to know, "If he had given up a possession of his recently?" Mario answered, "Yes, it was a trophy ring which I had won!" The Japanese Officer handed his ring back saying, "I was at that game and I saw the great run you made. I am pleased to return it to you but you had best keep it hidden because the next time it may not be returned to you."

Source: Charles Morrison, Notre Dame CL '38 and Martin Finnerty who as a youth grew up with Mario in the same Chicago neighborhood .

Lt. General Wainwright's Letter
Corregidor's Surrender May 5, 1942

L t. General Jonathan M. Wainwright carefully surveyed the situation of Corregidor Island Fortress in Manilla Bay. Since the Japanese attack on December 7, 1941, the enemy had pursued aggressive action throughout the South Pacific which included the 10th of December attack on the Philippine Island of Luzon. The Filipinos and American Forces had fought delaying action to prevent the capture of the Bataan Peninsula. The delaying action bought time to repair ships at Pearl, recruit and train men to now defend their country. But without replenishments of food, malaria pills and ammunition there comes the hard question of what is best for your gallant men who are willing to continue against such odds. They had fought uncomplainingly the steady bombardment, air attacks and mortar fire for ninety days. On April 9, 1942 with heads bloody but unbowed, the Bataan Peninsula unit of the American-Filipino Army under Major General Edward P. King, USA yielded to a greater force and well equipped and supplied enemy.

However on the "Rock," known, as Corregidor, the remnants of the Fil-American armed forces under Lt. General Wainwright continued to resist the air attacks, and the wicked bombardment as long as there was ammunition. Without food or ammunition, with many men ill with tropical diseases, dysentery and no replenishments in sight, Wainwright realized Corregidor must yield. The submarine which brought in the last of replenishments in February withdrew with the gold bullion that stabilized the Philippine currency. There was no relief in sight. There was nothing more to protect or save except these proud, brave men.

On May 5th, 1942, Lt General Wainwright sent Presi-

dent Franklin D. Roosevelt his final wire, before going to meet with the Japanese Lt. General Masaharu Homma to arrange the terms of the surrender.
Excerpts from that radio wire are given here.

"There is a limit to human endurance and that limit has long since been past. Without prospects of relief, I feel it is my duty to my country and to my gallant troops to end this useless effusion of blood and human sacrifice.

"With profound regret and with continued pride in my gallant troops , I go to meet the Japanese Commander" (signed)

Lt. General Jonathan M. Wainwright, US Army

Note: The lyrics of "The Battling Bastards of Bataan" by Frank Hewlett, (1942) summarize the foot soldiers view of their embattled position.

We are the battling bastards of Bataan
No momma, no pappa, no Uncle Sam
No aunts, no uncles, no cousins, no nieces
No pills, no planes, no artillery pieces
And nobody gives a damn !

Source: Oral history, Bill Bragg and Military Magazine Vol. XX1 July 2004

Tokyo Rose – American Citizen
Also a POW Being Held in Tokyo, Japan

Tokyo Rose was a radio voice on the Japanese airwaves of the South Pacific. Her pronouncements sometimes gave military high commands concern over the near accuracy of her messages. Items of American military information that was supposed to be highly secret would be broadcast from her Japanese Air Station like as though she had attended the briefing. Much of her information touched on US Ships locations, change of command assignments and other information on military maneuvers that were supposedly secret. She also issued disturbing messages for the South Pacific American troops.

Prior to her Japanese propaganda releases she would play the music of the 1940's. The ship's crews could hear the popular music performed by Benny Goodman, Tommy Dorsey or Artie Shaw. At Christmas time we listened to Bing Crosby's " White Christmas." Most ship's Communications department with the Commanding Offices approval, would put her broadcasts on the 1-MC circuit.

This is the main communication circuit and it reaches every living compartment on the ship. In fact this is the circuit on which the orders like "All-Hands-Man-your-Battle-Stations" or "Abandon-ship" would be received. The music was well received and every shipmate would have pleasant recollections of home, a girl friend, a wife or the last big band at a USO party he attended. Then following the good music would come information such as, where a certain USS Carrier was, or what island a Battleship was anchored near. Also we heard an Admiral was recently seen in Tulagi or some South Pacific location. Mostly false information but sometimes very close to the truth.

For the crews, she would tell them *"that your girl friend is doing some heavy dating with a 4-F fellow who has just moved into the neighborhood!"* Stories like this and others were so far fetched from reality that an enjoyable laugh would break up the day and the monotony of a daily task.

It must have had some disconcerting effect on the high commands because a Navy Memo was issued directing all Port Authorities to **"not report the arrival or departure of Major War Vessels."** This memo ended up with confusion for the Port Authorities in Leyte Gulf in the case of the *USS Indianapolis.* The *USS Indy* failed to meet her arrival date and nothing was done or said as to where she was. Five days later, after failing her estimated time of arrival (ETA), several ships were sent to investigate unknown objects in the Philippine Sea. It was then learned, that only 317 men of a crew of 1197 survived the *USS Indianapolis* sinking.

It wasn't until after the surrender of Japan that the facts about Tokyo Rose were learned. She was an American daughter whose Japanese parents had become Naturalized American citizens. Her birth name was "Iva Ikuko Toguri Daquino." She was born in America and graduated in 1941 from a California University. Her graduation present was a trip to Tokyo but she had to wait until the fall farm crops were harvested before the money would be available to send her. Late in November 1941 she went to visit her grandparents and cousins in the Tokyo area. Her return to the United States was denied by the Japanese government and she was kept in Japan for propaganda purposes. Since she was educated, and read and spoke both English and Japanese, she was forced to broadcast the Japanese propaganda releases prepared by Japanese War Lords.

After the war Tokyo Rose was arrested, tried for treason and convicted. She was sentenced to 10 years in a Federal Penitentiary, plus a fine of $10,000. She was released on parole after 6 years. Given a chance again to clear her name, she stated the true situation she found herself in after the Pearl Harbor attack. We learned she was a POW in Japan and forced to proclaim the various scripts prepared for her on her radio broadcasts. If she didn't cooperate, her newly met grandparent's lives were in jeopardy. Many years later President Gerald Ford, on the last day of his Presidential term, granted her a pardon. She also, being a Prisoner of War, is recognized in this chapter.

Source: Alligator Alley News Letter dated May 2003 #51 page 15. This writer's actual shipboard listening experience.

Chapter Four

Ensign Talman Meets Churchill Again
Haul Down that Flag

Ensign Talman and the *USS Wichita*
Circle Up The Wagons

Colonel Lewis Held's Report
The Biak Incident

Colonel Lewis Held Reports
"Hari-Kiri" in the Hebrides

Dr. Samuel Billison, Private 1st Class, US Army
Navajo Code Talkers

Ensign Talman Meets Churchill Again
Haul Down that Flag

It is January 6, 1943 and the *USS Wichita* is on station in company with the *USS Chicago* departing Noumea and en route with a screen of Destroyers toward Efate to establish a new staging base. This will put the Fleet Headquarters 700 miles north of Noumea and 200 miles south of the Solomon Islands. While anchored in Efate Atoll, Ensign Talman's promotion to Lt.(jg) has arrived by Navy Alnav. The new Lieutenant has the in-port watch and a message is received to "stand by to receive visitors." The small air speck in the eastern blue sky registers "Friendly" on the IFF scope. (Identification Friend or Foe) There is no indication who the visitors on the PBM (Mariner) are. In the atoll lagoon a smooth air landing is effected and the aircraft motors right up to the outboard slung gangway to accommodate the visitors arrival. It is a short bulky figure making his way up the ladder that causes Lt.(jg) Talman to stare in disbelief. By his gate and chomped-on cigar, there is no doubt it is Winston Churchill, who is followed by Fleet Admirals Nimitz and Halsey.

The messenger of the watch and the marine guard are hurriedly dispatched to alert the senior officers aboard who the arriving guests are. Admiral Halsey is the last to step on the after deck and he does so with a firm command of,

"Haul down that Ensign !"

Well the OOD (Officer on Deck) has three ensigns (flags) flying and doesn't know which one should be hauled down. His ship the *USS Wichita*, has just joined the South Pacific fleet and is unaware of what appears to be a small housekeeping matter of which a Fleet Admiral should not be bothered. In fact there are three ensigns now flying on the ship. The American flag is called an ensign and flies at the main mast, a smaller one is on the jack staff aft indicating the ship is anchored, and the third is the "Starred" ensign on the starboard halyard indicating that Fleet Admiral Robert C. Giffen is aboard. Admiral Halsey spoke again saying, *"Get Admiral Giffen's flag down immediately!"*

Lt (jg) Talman calls the signal bridge and directs the Admiral's flag be lowered. Later it is learned that there is an order in the South Pacific for the "Flag Officers" not to fly their ensigns. The Japanese pilots are directed to watch for the ships flying them, as this is the place where the enemy leadership exists. If this leadership can be destroyed the enemy ships will be less effective in the war.

USS *Wichita* receives visitors.
OOD told — "Haul down the Ensigh!"

That evening after the movie on the spacious after deck which was attended by the visitors, Lt.(jg) Talman had a chance to visit with Mr. Churchill. In their chat, Talman informed Mr. Churchill, that he was one of the four Ensigns who visited him at 10 Downing Street, London. He also told him about the four Ensigns who left two sections of the Royal palace Guard of Buckingham Palace at attention and never returned the Royal Salute they were offered. Mr Churhill had learned about it and found it humorous to meet one of those Ensigns.

Ensign Talman and the
USS Wichita
Circle Up The Wagons

It was 29 January 1943 the *USS Wichita*, in company with the *USS Chicago* with a screen of Destroyers, is escorting a group of Transport Ships to Guadalcanal. At twilight the convoy was attacked by a group of Japanese torpedo bombers. The alerted crew comes quickly to their General Quarters stations and they bring their guns to bear on the enemy aircraft. The 5" x 38 " guns are using the powder canisters from their Atlantic Ocean War which are not the "flashless" powder type. This means the powder charge put behind the 5-inch bullets to propel the bullets causes the gun crews to readjust their eyes after every bullet is fired. Said another way, the gun crews are temporarily blinded by the flash and it takes a few minutes for their eyes to adjust before the next shot can be fired accurately.

The Japanese Torpedo bombers must drop low to launch their torpedoes and in doing so they realizing the gun crews are blinded. Knowing this they fly low longer to allow their machine guns to spray the gun crews before they elevate their flight over the ships. Recognizing the problem Lt.(jg) Talman orders his gun crews to take cover behind the gun shields. In his writings he wrote, *"he could hear the enemy bullets bouncing off the gun shields around the gun crews."*

The *USS Chicago* was positioned behind the *USS Wichita* in the convoy. Unfortunately the Chicago takes three torpedo hits and the hope of saving her is futile. The Chicago crew is abandoning ship as best they can as the ship rolls to the starboard side and rapidly capsizes. Quickly Wichita's Admiral Giffen orders all ships to form a circle behind him, to increase their speed to flank and to turn on their searchlights. Yep, you get it! He has gone "Cowboy" style to lessen the target value of every ship as they steam at their maximum speed in a circle. The lights illuminate the circle with the sinking Chicago and her abandoning crew in the middle of the circle. Also one of the Destroyers (*USS Lavalette*) is lost.

As a result of the circling Admiral Giffen was awarded a medal for his quick decision under stress. It was also noted that the Japanese Aircraft appeared to be confused by the forming of a circle. The circle made it easier to recover a large percent of the sailors who abandoned ship. These sailors would man the fighting ships again. But best of all the Japanese flyers lost track of the Transport ships with the circle movement and all Transports arrived safely at Guadalcanal.

The *USS Wichita* was ordered back to an ammunition ship in Efate to replace the Atlantic Ocean load of powder canisters with the correct flashless powder canisters. They also learned that Wichita's Captain Low had sighted four torpedoes and maneuvered to escape three of them. The forth struck the ship but failed to explode. This reminded Lt. (jg) Talman of a possible earlier one that sent the Wichita to the Scotland Ship Yard when the Wichita was part of the "Brits" Home Fleet.

Source: *USS Wichita* (CA 45) from Carter Talman's *Memoirs of World War II Highlights of the USS Wichita*, June 30, 1945

Colonel Lewis Held's Report
The Biak Incident

Biak is a small island off the Northwest corner of New Guinea and part of the Dutch East Indies Island Group. A sizeable Allied Airport was established here and flights to and from this Island were frequent. Its location was ideal for making passage to the East as well as further West. Colonel Held was here with orders waiting to catch a flight East. Having orders gave him a "priority seat" for the next available flight out. Though Biak was considered a secured airbase, anti-aircraft batteries still guarded the runways and base operations. There were occasional incidents with an occasional Japanese fighter planes but the threat of any real attack was slim or next to none.

While waiting for the next flight East, Colonel Held was approached by the Base Commander asking if he would consider giving up his "priority seat" for a Marine whose father was dying in the States. Colonel Held readily agreed to relinquish his seat knowing that he might not catch a flight going to his destination until the next day. Colonel Held watched the airplane load and wished the Marine a quick flight home to see his dad. Then stepping back into the flight operations building he watched the aircraft take off and climb in the eastward sky. Suddenly a Japanese "Zero" appeared and just as suddenly there was a puff of smoke in the sky. Then a thin trail of smoke followed as the passenger aircraft plunged down into the ocean. All on board perished.

Colonel Held spoke with the Operations Officer who had pulled out the manifest which lists the names of those aboard. Death notices could be deferred on some of those aboard but the Marine's family had been informed that their son had luckily caught a flight and was on his way home. There are no easily written telegraph wires informing a family who was losing a father that they have now lost a son. The Operations Officer, with a deep sigh said, *"I have lost a pilot, and his co-pilot, a fine air crew and a much needed aircraft. Now I must write those families also."*

Colonel Held stood there quietly with the Operations Officer as he tried to regain his composure. Stepping back from that emotional moment, Colonel Held thanked his God who had guided his decision to give up that "priority seat." In a war zone death is always close and prayers are often said.

Source: Lewis Held's memoirs as provided by his son, Lewis I Held, Jr.

Colonel Lewis Held Reports
"Hari-Kiri" in the Hebrides

Col. Lewis Held flew to the New Hebrides Base to check on conditions there. On about his second night, he was awaked at 3:30 am by one of his Aides and was told that something strange was going on in the stockade where the 39 Japanese P.O.W.'s were being held. Dressing quickly he strapped on his pistol and proceeded with the Aide to investigate the "strange problem."

When he entered the first tent he found that all three Japanese prisoners had hung themselves using the tent ropes. They had stood on boxes, which they had kicked out from under their feet. Before doing so they had disemboweled themselves or slit their throats by using their mess spoons with one edge sharpened into razor sharpness. In front of each man was a seashell which had been somehow collected. In each shell was a smoldering cigarette butt in an attempt to represent a ritual candle for suicide. In going to the next 12 tents, Colonel Held witnessed the same sadistic sight. All of the 39 had hung themselves   All but one were already dead.

Through an interpreter, the last survivor, before he died, explained that by surrendering instead of fighting to their death, they had brought disgrace and dishonor upon themselves. (It was believed they were captured without their weapons). They could never return to their homes so there was nothing for which to live.

Colonel Held was called by his Commanding General to make a full report, and the General, in turn, had to file a report in Washington, D.C. Rumors had been getting back to the States that United States troops "did not take prisoners." that is, they killed them. The lone survivor's explanation proved that the rumor of not taking prisoners was false. The practice of "*hara-kiri*" indicated the attitude of the Japanese toward surrendering. If the invasion of Japan by the Allies occurred in order to bring a close to the war, the loss of Japanese lives would have been astronomical. This self-sacrificing view held by Japanese Nationals during WW II was not known or understood by those who criticized the Hiroshima bomb.

In another writing in this book there is the statement by a marine saying when looking down into the Japanese trenches, *"The only good Jap is a dead Jap!"* Perhaps this led to the thinking that we took no prisoners which is not true. Above is the true story of the imprisoned Japanese Nationals who believed *"hara-kiri"* was the proper course of action if captured. Later in this book the reader will learn of the suicide action on Tinian and Saipan Islands where families with small children took similar action. Also the reader will learn how a "Bull Horn" saved many Japanese Nationals.

Source: Memoirs of Colonel Lewis I. Held, US Army

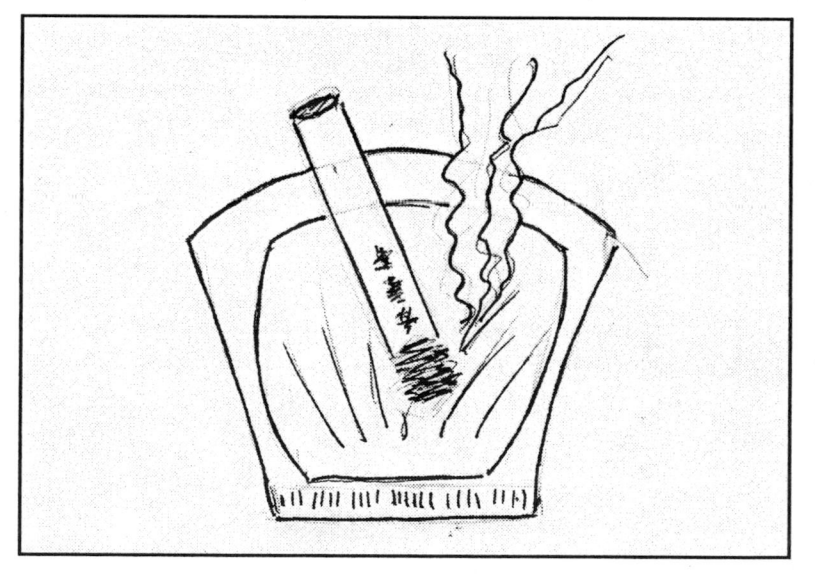

Shell and lit cigarette acting as a voltive ritual candle for
Hari Kiri suicide.

Dr. Samuel Billison's
Navajo Code Talkers

November 20, 2003

D r Samuel Billison, a native American Indian of the Navajo Tribe possesses both BA and MA degrees from the University of Oklahoma and has a Doctorate in Philosophy from the University of Arizona. He was the guest speaker at a meeting at the Richmond, Virginia McGuire Veteran's Hospital. In the audience was the narrator with another Richmond, Va. Navy Leaguer.

This is a synopsis of that speech concerning the development of the Navajo code which aided the war effort in WWII in the Pacific Ocean Areas. After greeting us Dr. Billison opened his remarks with the following.

Navajo Code Talkers send, receive and interpret message in less than two minutes

"If we didn't win the war, we would be eating a lot of rice!"
The audience chuckled with laughter. When asked why, as
a Navajo Indian youth, did he join the Marines. He answered, **"Our mother country had been attacked!"** The Marine recruiting signs struck him as the type of warrior he
wished to be. He tried to join when he was 16 but the Marine recruiter said it best if he stayed in High School until
he graduated. Not wanting to wait, he was able to convince
his mother to sign for him when he was 17. Once enlisted,
he was assigned to the San Diego Marine Corps with 29
other Navajo Indians in the recruited group. Upon completion of basic training he was reassigned to a special group
now being located in Oceanside, California. The reason-
ing behind this is as follows.

Unlike the Cherokee Nation which has a written and
an oral language, the Navajo does not have a written language. The language is communicated by either a pho-
netic nasal or guttural sound or by the pitch or a tone sound.
Depending on how the sound is expressed is the meaning
of the word in use.

The military had need for a quicker translation of messages in a battle areas. A military message sent then, had to
have time-date lines, a priority indicator, such as routine,
priority or urgent affixed to the message. Not every decoding location had the necessary decoding devices that would
permit the message's rapid decoding. Often it took two to
three hours to get the message decoded. Semiphore and
blinker light (Aldis Lamp) were easily read by the enemy.
Using the Navajo code a message could be decoded and
relayed in two minutes.

The Japanese were very gifted in breaking the American code. This is illustrated in the example in the Battle
of Midway. The Japanese intercepted a "phony" Naval
message indicating a lack of fresh water on Midway. The
Naval Forces issued the encoded messages saying,

" they doubted Naval Forces could defend
Midway because of the lack of fresh water. "

When intercepted and decoded, the Japanese sent their fleet to Midway expecting a cake walk but they met our Naval Forces and suffered the loss of several Japanese Carriers and their pilots. The Midway battle became the turning point of the Pacific War.

When graduated the 29 Navajo Marines, now all Privates 1st Class were sent to the Oceanside California barracks. Here they were placed in a room, the door was closed and they were instructed to develop a code. It must be verbally communicated and understood when received. The Navajo took each letter of the alphabet and put that letter in three areas. The areas were – AIR, GROUND and SEA.

For Example: *The Air —*

Alphabet Word	Indian Word	Meaning
gini	chicken hawk –	dive bomber
*da-he-tih-hi	humming bird	fighter plane

The Ground —

*chay-da-gahi	*tortoise–	or tank
*ah-zhol	no Indian word	bazooka

The Sea —

ca-lo	shark–	Destroyer
besh-lo	iron fish	Submarine

Further the letter "A" like all alphabet letters was assigned three different words in the code. wolachee = "ant," tsenill ="axe" and belasana = "apple"

Thirteen of the original group were spread among various islands in the South Pacific. Two were kept to teach the code in the Oceanside location. Each of the Island groups hereafter listed received two code talkers. One to send the message and the other to receive and translate. Guadalcanal, the Marshall, Solomon Islands, Saipan and Iwo Jima each received two code talkers. Guam received three code talkers.

One code talker was captured during the war and was transferred to a Tokyo prison. As a Prisoner of War, he was shown Navajo code words the Japanese had recorded and directed him to translate. He told them the meaning of the Navajo words. He was punished and put back in prison. After the war when he was released the code talker revealed what had happened to him.

When the war ended the "code talkers" were instructed to never reveal the meanings of the code and to never talk about it to anyone. In 1982 the code was declassified after having remained unbroken all these years. Today, Dr Billison said the messages are transferred by laser beam and can be read with in seconds. The Navajo code is no longer used.

There were 421 code talkers and about 75–100 exist today. They are spread over a wide area and it is difficult to stay in contact with them as many are back at their old occupation as shepherds tending sheep. Of the 29 original code talkers, five are still living and only four attended their recognition ceremony on November 24, 2001.

When they were discharged from the Marine Corps **some** were awarded a Gold medal said to be worth $33,000. The others received a Silver medal but they never told the value of the medal. They remained as Privates First Class all during their service time. They were mustered out of the Marine Corps as Corporals but never received pay as such.

To this day, Dr. Billison said the Navajo carry a "**corn pod**" which is taken from the top of an ear of corn near where the pollen is located. It is a fetish and used as a form of prayer. The prayer goes in this manner. Step one–touch fetish top and then the tongue. Step two–touch the fetish top and then touch the head. Step three–touch the fetish top then touch the ground. The Holy People of the Navajo tribe also use it in fertility prayers with regard to the sky, earth and water. Fertility is there when all are in harmony.

In his talk Dr. Billison said the "Code talkers" brought "Peace and Unity" to their land by enlisting in the Marine Corps. They were the "**majestic voices**" of the South Pacific reported to have saved over 200,000 lives. To this day they are United States Marines and their land is the United States of America.

The meeting was closed with a prayer. This included the sounding of an Indian drum and chanting. Another speaker interpreted the Navajo prayer being chanted. To the listener there were high notes, nasal notes and low notes with the drum amplifying and modulating the sounds. The interpretation was "a thank you to their God and a wish for their God to continue his blessing on this land called The United States of America.

Source cited in this report.

Chapter Five

Pearl Harbor Revisited
by Patricia F. Nagle

The Sea Bees–The Unsung Heroes

A Seventeen-Year-Old Veteran
Andy Nazario

USS *Callaghan* Stories by M. Moreau

Tinian Island Stories
Tuffy & the Bull Horn
Synopsis of Lt Cliff Graham's Article
M/Sgt Curley Klabo Recognized
The 509th Air Group–B-29 Base on Tinian Island

Bruno Shuster's Secret

Pearl Harbor Revisited
by Patricia F. Nagle

December 07, 2001

Pearl Harbor's name is derived from "pearl oysters" which grew in the Pearl Stream flowing seaward on the southern shore of Oahu Island. Oahu is part of the Hawaiian Island Group. In 1887 the Hawaiian Government and the United States entered an agreement establishing Pearl Harbor as a "coaling station" for the Pacific Fleet. Steam ships were coming to the fore over the sailing vessels and coal stations were necessary. The Pearl Harbor has three "lochs" which is an English word for lakes and are designated as East Loch, West Loch and Central Loch. These "lochs" with shallow depths are the nesting areas for the smaller US war vessels. Ford Island located near the center provided deeper water for mooring Battleships. This was known as Battleship Row. In the early days before the Pearl Harbor attack, the then Naval Commandant of Pearl Harbor, Admiral Richardson, became an irritant to President F. D. Roosevelt because he felt only FDR could and should authorize a change of location for the Battleships.

Admiral Richardson complained and urged that one half of the US Battleships be home based in a West Coast port. He was concerned that the eight Battleships were so closely berthed in the Battleship Row that they presented an easy target. President Roosevelt in order to stop the insistent drum beat requesting that the Battleship fleet be divided into two parts, had Admiral Richardson relieved as Commandant of Pearl Harbor in February 1941, just ten months before the Japanese attack. His replacement was Admiral Husband E. Kimmel, USN

Pearl Harbor had two attacks occurring at 7:53 am, 8:55 am on December 7, 1941. By 9:55 am the attacks were all over and the Japanese fleet was departing the area. The *USS Nevada* was the only Battleship of the eight present in Battleship Row able to slip her moorings and head to sea. The seven others were either sunk or severely damaged. The *USS Arizona* was sunk with the loss of 1177 crewmembers due to Japanese torpedo hits and explosions of her ammunition magazines. Ship's Officer. LCdr Fuqua was able to save over 200 of the Arizona crew by his quick action. Here is his story as I have been told by LCdr Fuqua's daughter, Mrs. Patricia Fuqua Nagle.

On Saturday December 6, 1941, Lt. Kelly was the *USS Arizona*'s Watch Officer and invited his wife and daughters to come aboard and join him for dinner in the Officer's Wardroom. LCdr Fuqua was also aboard but his family was stateside. As a thoughtful gesture LCdr Fuqua offered to relieve Lt Kelly of the watch so Lt Kelly could spend the night with his family on the beach. Lt. Kelly accepted, thanked Fuqua and the watch question was settled. LCdr Fuqua decided to bunk topside in the space provided for the duty Watch Officer. This decision probably saved his life as he was able to direct those men available topside to aid many of those below to escape the sinking. Later he was awarded the "Medal of Honor" for his quick action and leadership in saving over 200 crewmembers.

Several days after the *USS Arizona* sinking, LCdr Fuqua, dressed in diving gear, worked his way down to his sunken quarters to retrieve some of his personal belongs. While in his diving gear, as he entered his compartment he noted his uniforms on the hangers, swaying back and forth in the flooded waters of his compartment. He recovered most of his personal items including his sword.

Now as a sidelight the sword is an interesting piece of uniform accoutrement. This I learned from Mrs. Patricia F. Nagle. When her dad was a Naval Academy Midshipman, a Frenchman was part of the instructional staff. The additional subjects taught by the French Instructor were dancing and sword handling. The footwork of dancing was considered very essential when wielding a sword. The earlier days of Naval warfare required repelling boarders through the use of the sword. It was a very important art that must be learned. Today the sword, though still part of a Naval Uniform, is a symbol of authority and basically ceremonial.

Now back to Pearl Harbor during WW II, as I recall a wooden platform was built over one of the sunken gun casements of the *USS Arizona* on which a very tall flag steel pole was raised. Every morning before the 0800 bugle call two sailors would row out to the platform to raise the American flag. "Attention to colors" was piped over the loud speaker from the Pearl Operations Base and the colors would be raised with the playing of the National Anthem. We would all come to attention where we stood, facing the flag, and salute.

During WW II and in the Korean War as our ship departed Pearl Harbor, making passage through the channel heading toward the sea, we passed that wooden platform with the flag at the peak of the pole. With a signal from our ship's bridge, all hands come to attention and hold a hand salute, thereby rendering honors to starboard as we pass this site. The American flag at the peak snaps sharply in the morning breeze. The lanyards flap against the metal pole in a rhythmic meter that seem to me to say, "Pray, for us! Pray, for us!" On the water there is a sheen of oil still seeping from the sunken Arizona which seems to serve as a balm calming our emotions but also setting our wills to steel. We know why we were underway. Our generation again in 1950, was called to return to the Pacific for the Korean War. Again we pass this site, render honors and sail forth to bring peace to this blue ocean.

Today, (the 60th anniversary) the wooden platform has

been replaced by the Monument which straddles the *USS Arizona*'s sunken hull. Today also, the *USS Missouri* a 1944 WW II Battleship, is moored nearby. When we stand in the Monument over the *USS Arizona*'s sunken hull and view the *USS Missouri*, we are with the ships signifying the beginning and ending of WWII. The Monument has a large engraved marble wall listing those who were lost with the USS Arizona's sinking. On the *USS Missouri* there is well-polished brass plate marking the spot where the Japanese surrender occurred on September 2, 1945.

On the 60th anniversary December 07, 2001, my wife Helen and I joined Mr. & Mrs. Charles (Patricia Fuqua) Nagle in Pearl Harbor. There with the living survivors of *USS Arizona* we found good fellowship and camaraderie. We gathered and reviewed the ships, the cemetery and the museum. When we visited the museum, there on one wall was LCdr Fuqua's picture, his Medal of Honor citation and below the picture and citation was his sword. His dancing footwork and sword-wielding days have been put to rest. Boarders come now to pay their respects and we thank God for men like him.

L. Peter Wren, LCDR USNR (ret)
Richmond, Virginia

Source: Mrs. Patrica Fuqua Nagle
Book–*The United States Navy*, 1986 by Capt. Edw. L. Beach, USN
USS Arizona, Reunion Assoc. Newsletter, December 2004

The Sea Bees–
The Unsung Heroes

The day of depending on the sail and the wind for a US Naval Force disappeared with the introduction of the steam engine. The question then rose as to where will the fuel be found to make the steam that will propel the Naval vessels across the Pacific vast ocean? The Pacific theater of war is filled with coral islands dotted with palm trees which supply nothing of use as a source of power. All of the above proves that "Necessity is the mother of invention!" And that takes us to the US Naval Construction Battalions or in the short title called **CBs**. A gifted illustrator envisioned them as a **Bee** wearing a Navy white hat and carrying a construction man's tools and a gun. Of course being Navy oriented, they would have to reflect something in their name to indicate their sea-going prowess. So "C" of construction rhymes with "Sea" and there you have it.

The concept of the Sea Bees was to develop forward bases from which the war could be fought by providing storage fuel for ships and aircraft, food and housing for crews, a saltwater conversion ability, roads, docks and piers, airstrips, repair facilities, hospitals and rest camps for the injured and ill. This in itself is a very large order in view of the wide expanse of the Pacific Ocean, It also would be necessary for the Sea Bees to be able to man the guns and fight. Thus came the Sea Bee Motto–"**Can Do!**" which is followed by their "Fight song."

Here is the first verse,

**We are the Sea Bees of the Navy,
And we can build and we can fight,
And we will pave our way to Victory,
And guard it day or night !** etc.

After all the Navy and Marines had a fight song so it was just keeping up with military spirit.

The first group of Naval Construction troops, called the **"Bob Cats"** were ordered in January 1942 to Bora Bora in the Societies Islands. The naming appears to be a simple case of reversing the letters **CB** to **BC**. However the "Sea Bees" was the final choice of a moniker. At Bora Bora their job was to build a fueling station and a Naval Base that would serve the ships as a near supply center while enroute to Australia or the Solomon Islands. We needed to get a toehold in the South Pacific and a refueling and rearming station was a first priority. Also islands with an air base would make an ideal unsinkable carrier from which to launch our road to Tokyo. The Sea Bees were a proud group of construction men recruited for their "know how" and outside of a little military training they could build anything, anywhere the Navy placed them.

The 1st Battalion of Sea Bees was ordered to the New Hebrides in August 1942 near where the Japanese were trying to build an airstrip on one of the islands named Guadalcanal. Hawthorn D. Nicholls of Richmond, Virginia, was with this First Battalion. Nicholls is now age 93 and has memories of those early days which he shared with this narrator. Also in Richmond, Virginia is Captain James Mims who supplies several CB stories of note in this book. Other known local Sea Bees, now deceased are E. M. "Mac" Crush, Ralph Williams, and Linwood Garrett who over the years have related their CB experiences to the author.

In the Hebrides Islands the Sea Bees, because of their know how and special equipment, finished the air field the Japanese were building. Our fighter planes flew quickly off the Hebrides airfield and rained bombs on the Japanese construction efforts on Guadalcanal Island. When we captured Guadalcanal the Japanese airfield was nowhere near completion. Trying to drive us off Guadalcanal the Japanese continued to bomb what we now called Henderson field. The flight plans of the Japanese bombers were so routine that the Sea Bees had an assembly line organized to handle the damage. Known was, how much sand and gravel would be needed to fill the bomb holes. The CB's bulldozers and dump trucks were loaded, ready and placed on the sides of the airfield. The "CBs had also placed the metal Marston mats nearby for easy repair. Marston Mats sustain the weight of the airplanes and helped level the field. After the Japanese bomb attack the Sea Bees would scramble from their trenches and quickly restore the airfield. Our aircrafts were able to land, refuel and take off again. The Japanese never caught the American aircraft on the ground.

The group of construction workers, called "Bob Cats," were transferred from Bora Bora to augment the 1st Battalion of Sea Bees in the Hebrides Islands. Upon arrival the Bob Cats were greeted by 1st Battalion of CB's with flapping their arms along side of their bodies and making a buzzing sound from their mouths. Eventually the Bob Cats merged into the 1st Battalion of Sea Bees.

One of the many areas where the Sea Bees performed well was on the Island of Guam. My first experience was when our ship tied up to the pier built in Guam's Apra Harbor. Without the breakwall, the mooring required constant surveillance of the lines securing the ship to the pier. Ocean wave surges flowed fully at the pier. This meant constant handling of the mooring lines as the ship rose and fell away from the pier with each wave. Upon completion of the break wall Apra Harbor became a strong source of Naval supplies.

Through Apra Harbor the bullets, bread, butter , bombs and bandages all made their way to sustain the fighting forces. Near the war's end the Guam hospital and medical facilities built by the Sea Bees lessened the long flight to Pearl Harbor and thereby reduced the risk to the wounded of delayed medical care. The survivors from the *USS India-napolis*, and the wounded from the fierce battles of Okinawa and Iwo Jima received almost instant medical help at the Guam hospital. The long flight of the wounded to Pearl Harbor, would have overloaded the Pearl Medical Facilities. The Sea Bees were certainly unsung heroes. Many a military man was saved by their quick construction and know how.

Guam is the largest island in the Marianas. There are other Islands just north of Guam that were put to great use to aid the war effort. The Construction Battalion's "Can Do" on the islands of Saipan and Tinian Island will follow when you read of the B-29 bombers.

Source: Oral histories by those mentioned in this writing

A Seventeen-Year-Old Veteran
Andy Nazario

The story of Andy Nazario is not too different from the many teenagers who volunteered for military service before finishing high school. A very large portion of the depression babies born in 1928 joined the military with the permission of their parents. His story is as follows:

It was Sunday, December 7, 1941 and Andy Nazario, age 14, was helping his dad repair an automobile belonging to a staff member of a local New England Hospital. Inside the unheated barn next to the Hospital power plant Andy watched and fetched tools as his dad labored on that Sunday morning. The peace of the morning was shattered when an engineer from the power plant ran into the barn informing them of the Pearl Harbor bombing. Pearl Harbor in the Hawaiian Islands became a new word in Andy's vocabulary. Little did he know that with a short span of years he would be in the Navy seeing first hand the wrecked and sunken American ships in Pearl Harbor.

With his mother's signature, Andy was accepted into the Navy and was shipped from Boston to the new Naval Training Station in Sampson, NY. This was followed by equipment training in Davisville, Rhode Island. Here he trained with the Construction Battalions, then known as the Sea Bees (CB's). Shortly after this he received orders to report to his first ship on the west coast. Six days later, traveling by train, he arrived in San Francisco. He would get his "sea legs" aboard the *USS Calusa*, (APA 74) a troop transport. He was assigned a bunk, placed his gear in storage and went up on deck to see San Francisco fade on the horizon as his ship was enroute to Pacific war theater.

There were many troops aboard and the Pacific wasn't calm once they left the shadow of the Golden Gate Bridge.

The crowded living compartments, below the main deck, were permeated with the odors of nauseous retching men. Finding himself with a queasy stomach he received help from a friendly cook who gave him a lemon to suck on. That seemed to quiet his nauseous urges. The USS *Calusa* was a part of a convoy and was constantly changing course in a "Zigzag pattern." Depending on the ships heading, Andy Nazario didn't know whether he liked the "Zig" or the "Zag" best for his queasy stomach.

Upon arrival In Pearl Harbor, Andy was reminded of the Sunday morning when he first learned the name of this harbor. Now he sees the sunken vessels and he knows why he joined the Navy. The stay in Pearl Harbor was short but busy with training, loading stores and refueling. On the ship's departure from Pearl Harbor a scheduled gunnery practice was arranged with a friendly aircraft from Pearl Harbor. This aircraft would tow a target sleeve 100 feet behind the aircraft. On the pilots first pass down the starboard side of the USS Calusa some of the eager men on the guns were firing ahead of the towing aircraft. The pilot seeing the tracer bullets in front of his aircraft changed course and headed back to Pearl Harbor. The men on the portside guns were miffed because they never got a shot off.

It took about 30 days using the "zigzag" before they reached a small island in the Marianas group, called Tinian. The Island is about six miles long and about two and a half miles wide. There were some small mountains with some cliffs about 80 feet above the sea. These cliffs would prove to be the site of a horrible tragedy. Just north, about three miles, is the Island of Saipan where the war was ensuing. Tinian was still smoldering but considered secured. There were Japanese troops still hiding in the caves and in the jungle areas. Andy wrote, *"As we came into the landing area I saw a dead Japanese sniper still hanging in his tree position. The many cave mouths were strewn with dead Japanese and there were more dead inside the caves. We found the best way to get the live enemy out of the caves was by the flamethrower or to pour gasoline down through the vent holes and then drop a hand grenade after pulling the pin. He wished they would surrender rather than face this fiery death.* "

Andy Nazario's writings continue: *"My job with the Construction Battalion was on heavy duty equipment and I always kept my carbine near. I pulled a burial duty for a fellow named Martin and I was sad to see his body in a gun crate for a coffin. I was on the rifle squad and we fired a three volley of seven guns at his burial. This is part of rendering full honors to the deceased"*

Tinian Island 1944

Andy gave more details from a newspaper clipping without a heading which I relate here. The need for air bases from the Marianas Islands was predicated on the B-29s now under construction states side. The B29s (Super Fortress), needed a lengthy and properly built runway to support the loaded B-29s. When completed the B29 could carry a 20,000-pound bomb load and fly to and return from the Japanese Islands making the round trip of 3000 miles. Tinian Island was basically made of coral with sugar cane fields in the flat areas. In order to construct a level airfield the coral had to be blasted and then bulldozed and rolled. At take off and on landing the dust generated by the B-29 was later overcome by asphalt. The end result included four 8500-9000 feet runways at North Field, and two 8,000 feet runways at West Field plus a fighter plane airstrip near west Field. .

The CB Mobile Unit #597 was the builder of these fields and was comprised of personnel coming from the 134th, 137th and 144th CB Battalions. They arrived on Island September 4th, 1944 and with their "Can Do" motto and had the Super Fortresses meeting flight schedules in less than a year.

Andy continues his writing: *"From the North Field of Tinian the B-29's are on a rapid flying pace. We are working around the clock so it is not unusual to see a B 29 crash at least once a day when taking off. The B 29's carry an eleven-man crew. A typical load is thirty-six 500 lbs bombs, several tons of aviation gasoline, ammunition for the guns to fight off the Japanese zeros they encounter and oxygen for breathing at the high altitudes at which they fly. B-29's came weekly from the States to replace the losses. Some of the pilots only had about 200 flight hours with these big B-29's. There is a 'bone yard' for the B-29's that crashed at one end of this island."*

Japanese Home Lands are 1,500 miles distant and the flights are over open water all the way to the targets. The B-29's make a speed of 250 miles per hour providing there are no head winds. For one full month 24 hours a day the B-29's flew with fire bombs and anti-personnel bombs from Guam, Saipan and Tinian bombing Tokyo and any other Japanese city within their flight range.

Andy continues, *"One morning as I was driving my 4 X 4 truck to the harbor, I saw the USS Indianapolis at anchor."* (Note– This is July 26, 1945) Unknown to everyone then as to why the ship was there without escort, they learned later that two boxes (Little Boy and Fat Man) containing the "A Bombs" were unloaded and taken to North Field. These bombs were dropped on Hiroshima (Aug 6th, 1945) and Nagasaki (Aug 9th, 1945) and the Japanese surrendered on August 14, 1945. *"From this day forward,"* wrote Andy, *"the only date we cared to learn about was the date we were going back to the states."*

Sixty days after V-J day (September 2nd 1945) a transport was available and Andy Nazario joined 10,000 GI's, who were not so nauseous this time. There was no "zigzag plan" as homeward bound they steamed. Andy had seen Pearl Harbor, got his "Sea legs," saw the Enola Gay, the airship that flew the first atomic bomb, but his greatest thrill was sailing under the Golden Gate Bridge at the ripe old age of 18 coming home to the United States of America.

In order to introduce other articles emanating from Tinian Island Andy Nazario sent me several published articles he collected. He believed they would augment his story. Being a young military man he was always interested in what the other units on the Island were doing. The word **"scuttle butt"** should be introduced here to illustrate how the local news was transmitted. There was a newspaper on the island, but it was a very limited edition. A few pages were saved.

The frequent gathering place for the men was the local water cooler. The water cooler in Navy lingo is called the **"Scuttle butt."** Standing around and waiting for one's turn at the cooler was the spot where greetings and the news was exchanged. From the published articles some parts of the stories will be borrowed to give the reader a more comprehensive view of World War II in the South Pacific.

Source: Andy's writings. Miscellaneous loose news undated articles. *World Encyclopedia.* The narrator's knowledge of the *USS Indianapolis'* history.

Why was the *USS Indianapolis* acting like a cargo vessel?

USS *Callaghan* Stories
by M. Moreau

Here is another oral history of a 17-year-old World War Two sailor who sought the Navy Blue before his 18th birthday. The Navy recruiters knew by the time he finished "Boot Camp" he would be 18 and ready to put out to sea.

Marland Moreau was assigned to the *USS Callaghan*, DD 792, named after Admiral Daniel J. Callaghan who lost his life in the battle for Guadalcanal November 12, 1942. The *USS Callaghan*, newly commissioned, completed the "shake down cruise" and received orders to report to South Pacific on February 5, 1944. During the Naval Operations in the South Pacific the *USS Callaghan* received eight battle stars. The score board painted on the upper bridge bulkhead reflected 12 Japanese aircraft shot down, a like number for assisted kills, sunk one small Japanese coastal craft and rescued 6 of this Japanese crew. Also sunk one Japanese kaiten submarine. The kaiten submarine is a miniature submarine launched from a mother submarine.

Eight battle stars indicates the Destroyer was in the thick of the battles as it steamed close to the enemy's shores in support of the landing troops or was in a picket line of defense surrounding the Task Force of larger ships. Destroyers are the first line of defense for the Cruisers, Battlewagons and Carriers.

According to Marland Moreau, the *USS Callaghan* engaged in numerous shore bombardments but the real test of the ship's fighting ability came to the fore during the Okinawa invasion. The realization of death also was brought home to the ship's crew when a Japanese Kamikaze strafed the ship's after gun mount, wounding some but killing James McCann, a 19-year-old ship's baker. This was the ship's first war casualty and he was buried at sea. The burial at sea seemed to be so inadequate for a shipmate that greeted the ship's crew every morning with his fresh baked wares. He always baked at night because the ship's cooks had the ovens during the day. The crew was saddened and they missed his morning fares and his cheerful disposition.

In the air operations with the fleet, the *USS Callaghan* always took the rear guard plane station. This means positioning our ship 2000 yards to the rear and on the starboard quarter of the Carrier. The pilots coming back to land on the Carriers sometimes were running out of gas, or would be so badly shot up they could not make the landing. They would ditch in the sea near the stern of the Carrier. Here the *USS Callaghan* came into play recovering 17 of our American flyers who would fly again.

In one of the Kamikaze attacks there were 10 Japanese torpedo bombers, (called "Vals"), trying to break through the Destroyer's screen protecting the Carrier. We shot down three of them. After the Japanese planes were downed we search the area of their airplane's sinking for survivors just like we had for the sunken Japanese coastal vessel. There were none.

Earlier we brought aboard the six Japanese sailors from the sunken coastal vessel. They thought we would kill them, but that is not our nature. Some of the shorter statured sailors aboard offered their "work blue uniforms" to outfit these Japanese survivors with clothing. Since the Callaghan does not have a brig (think jail) aboard we proceeded to Iwo Jima Island and turned them over to the Marines stationed there. Shortly after this a "Time Magazine" came out showing two Marines holding guns on the six Japanese sailors who were wearing the Navy blue uniforms we had provided. The caption read, "Iwo Jima Marines Capture Japanese Sailors." Our Captain sent a wire informing the *Time Magazine* that the *USS Callaghan* had rescued these Japanese sailors after sinking their ship. These sailors were the six the *USS Callaghan* had saved after sinking their coastal vessel and were turned over to the Marines on Iwo Jima as "prisoners of war." A correction was never received from *Time Magazine* acknowledging the Captain's wire.

Another incident of interest has to do with a new young sailor who came aboard shortly after the "shake down cruise." It happened like this. A group of us had just finished breakfast and stepped out on the port deck to grab a smoke. "Lo and behold," there along side our ship was a periscope kicking up a rooster's tail of water. We hollered to the bridge but the Officer on watch kept looking too far out on the horizon for the periscope. Finally the Captain stuck his head over the port wing of the bridge and sighted the periscope. He ordered "Sonar Quarters" which is not the same as "General Quarters." This calls a special Sonar Team to take over the ship's operation for a submarine attack. Standard procedure at "Sonar Quarters" is to roll one depth charge from the depth charge rack with the explosion set for 200 feet. (Shallow setting). Also with the periscope so close to the ship, the standard procedure is to come about with the intention of ramming the submarine. In a tight circle with a depth charge set for 200 feet, the depth charge explosion is close to the ships hull. Sometimes this causes the ship's stern to surge up in the sea and sometimes the ship's side plates will quiver.

Well, now you have the picture. Our newest crewmember is on watch in the engine room. Never having experienced Sonar Quarters, he is startled, to say the least, with the exploding of the depth charge. Those of us who went through "shake down" are familiar with what takes place and even though disturbed, we remain at our stations. However our newest sailor is visibly very upset. Hand over hand, he raced up the ladder from the engine room to the main deck and then climbed two more ladders to the navigation bridge. There he found the Captain. He walked right up to him, poking his right index finger into the Captain's chest, he stated, "DON'T YOU EVER, EVER DO THAT AGAIN!" Then turning on his heel, he left the bridge area while the bridge crew looked on in utter amazement. The Captain, reflecting quietly, suddenly burst out laughing. He was quickly joined by the bridge crew.

The Kamikaze attacks at Okinawa were awesome. We had received orders that another Destroyer with newer equipment would replace us at 0800 hours July 29th, 1945. This was welcomed news because it meant we would be heading back to the States for a Navy Yard update. But unfortunately on a midnight kamikaze attack, the *USS Callaghan* received a fatal blow and it sunk at 0051 hours. This was just seven hours away from our release from the fleet. Marland Moreau was one of the fortunate sailors who escaped the sinking ship. He floated in the Philippine Sea for five and a half hours. By dawn he was rescued by the Destroyer due to relieve the Callaghan. He was not injured in the sinking, but not having a ship he spent a little time recuperating in Guam. On August 12, 1945 Moreau had his 20th birthday. The Japanese surrendered on the 15th of August 1945 and the surrender was signed on September 2, 1945.

Moreau, thanking the Lord, reflected that in just two short years of Naval service, he had crossed both the International Time Date line and the Equator becoming a member of the Golden Dragon Society and also was a proud "Shellback." He received several ribbons that supported battle stars. He was promoted to Radar man third class and stood his watches in the Combat Information Center. He lost a shipmate named McCann who was, like Moreau, one of the 19-year-old shipmates aboard.

Now the war was over but he recalls how he floated on the sea and worried about the sharks. He prayed for dawn's early light and rejoiced at dawn when he saw his flag proudly waving on the destroyer that was about to rescue him. He remembers the horror of the Kamikaze threat skimming over his ship and the loss of a 19-year-old shipmate. He remembers how they manned those picket lines placing their ship (Little Boys) in "Harms Way" to protect those (Big Boy) Cruisers, Battlewagon and Carriers. Best of all he is proud of the US Navy and of his service to his country. He truly enjoyed the bond of fellowship developed aboard the *USS Callaghan* (DD 792).

The only blue water he sees these days is Lake Huron which is one of the Great Lakes which flows leisurely under the Blue Water Bridge connecting Michigan's roads with Canadian roads. He loves to "spin" the story how a Seaman deuce issued the Captain a warning and never faced a Captain's Mast or even a "bread and water ration" for 30 days.

Source: Oral History as told by Marland Moreau with Destroyer Operations background added by LPW

Tinian Island Stories

B efore the reader can fully understand what the American Armed Forces encountered upon capturing the Japanese enemy or the Japanese civilians inhabiting the many Pacific Islands, a word of explanation is most desirable. Because of a Japanese National belief espoused by their leaders, the most honorable thing to do rather than be captured by the Americans was to end their lives either by suicide, "hara-kiri" or a "Banzi Attack" in which death was their desired result. These acts honored their family name. Anything less than these acts sullied all families good names forever. The first illustration of the Japanese mind set was given in the story told by Colonel Lewis Held while in the Hebrides Islands. (Chapter 4)

Through these pages the reader will come to fully understand this strange philosophy when you read the horrendous acts that loving parents committed with their beloved children. I say beloved children because I personally witnessed this love when we met the "Momma-sans and Poppa-sans" during the occupation days in 1945. The "Momma-sans and Poppa-sans" are the grandparents who raised the Japanese children orphaned by the war. Yes, as warriors we took some lives in battle but a lot more Japanese Nationals would have lived to come home had they surrendered rather than accepted "death for family honor" as the best answer.

The local Japanese families who made their homes on the Islands in the Marianas and the Japanese soldiers who were by-passed on these Islands were a tragedy waiting to happen because of this fanatic teaching. They believed that if they were captured by the Americans it would bring great dishonor to their family. They were told that Americans would eat their babies. This is why "hara-kari" was performed, or why suicide missions were so shockingly common.

Early in the war it was believed the American Forces did not take prisoners of war because there were no facilities to hold them in captivity, feed them and guard them from escape. Since the Japanese enemy were treacherous when alive the general feeling was "The best Jap was a dead Jap." Therefore calling or asking for their surrender was an act they never accepted. The Japanese warrior preferred the "banzi attack" to kill as many Americans as possible as he went to his death. The Japanese warrior shouted the abbreviated version of "*tenno heika banzai*" which means "may the Emperor live for 10,000 years." There just weren't any live Japanese survivors on the battlefields.

Tuffy and the Bull Horn

Tinian was reported secured but there still were pockets of Japanese soldiers fighting and resisting surrender. Tinian was the site of the new B-29 Airfields that the Sea Bees were building. This story comes to me from Andy Nazario undated newspaper clippings he sent. Given here are two of the stories.

Number One-

Three off-duty Sea Bees decided to explore the Tinian jungle that surrounded the airfield under construction. The area was considered safe and free of the former Japanese troops. So the Sea Bee buddies started to explore the jungle without their rifles and shortly thereafter came under fire by Japanese who were hiding in a nearby cave. Two of the three were killed instantly and the third, though wounded, did escaped. With that the Command decided that current method of trying to entice the remnant Japanese still hiding was not working. Burning out their caves with the flame throwers, as well as spreading flyers around in their language or calling out on a loud speaker by someone who could speak their language, wasn't working. The accents of the speakers were not Japanese and therefore not believed and surrenderings were not occurring.

A new method was devised and through some trickery the Americans captured about 14 of the hiding Japanese. They were provided comfortable quarters, food and medical care and the captives were asked to help convince their friends still in hiding to surrender. One of the captives appeared to be a leader and a tough one. The American nicked named him "Tuffy" and encouraged him to help bring others into the compound. The other captives respected Tuffy and did not treat him as a traitor. They all learned what the Americans promised was true and that their Emperor had mislead them. The American Command encouraged "Tuffy" to help stop the unnecessary killing of the Japanese troops in hiding. "Tuffy" was allowed to take a "Bull Horn" into the jungle area and encourage the remaining Japanese to come out. They turned him loose hoping that it would work. The evening of the first day he returned with eight be-draggled Japanese warriors for the compound. After few days in the compound, the newest prisoners were rested, well fed and convinced the Americans wanted to stop the unnecessary killing. Two of the recent captured group volunteered to work with "Tuffy." Soon this expanded to many volunteers.

After six weeks the volunteers had brought a total of 313 Japanese soldiers to the compound. Everyone of the volunteers return and none were looked on by their fellow prisoners as a traitor.

Number Two-

Lieutenant Cliff Graham's article published in *Coronet*

Magazine, June 01, 1945 and supplied by CB Andy Nazario. The *Coronet Magazine* is no longer in print but the story needs to be retold.

Tinian Island is now under American control and the Sea Bee's are constructing the B-29 airfields. Many Japanese civilian families and Japanese military personnel who have been living here were by-passed as the American War effort moves north. The Japanese parents, their children, plus the Japanese warriors are absolutely in great mortal fear of capture. This is a story of the American Forces attempting to save lives by asking those on a cliff to put aside the fanatical belief advanced by the Japanese Military leaders. They were taught "Death is preferable to surrender!" This is the 4th of August 1945 and it is two days before the Hiroshima Bomb is launched. A brief explanation of the situation follows.

Suicide Cliff Tinian Island

Our ship was close to the cliffs on the south side of Tinian so we could address the many Japanese soldiers and civilians collected together. There was a flat area with some caves nearby. The purpose of this operation was to stop the suicide action that was inspired by the false premises inculcated in Japanese minds by the fanatic military. It was dawn and we could see many families with babies and young children gathered together on the edge of the cliff. In the mouths of the caves many soldiers sat and stared back at us. Using binoculars we could see three soldiers stretched out on flat rocks with their stomachs laid open and oozing blood. Most likely "hara-kari" victims and slowly dying. Teenage girls and boys move around the rocks cautiously. Truly a gruesome sight of unnecessary deaths.

Our message was to this effect. "You cannot live there on the rocks without food and water. You should want to live and be happy. We have come to help you." They were urged to climb the slope of the cliff and walk to the north where the Marines would meet and guide them to a safe place. We maneuvered the ship nearer the cliff and around the point where we saw a group of young girls. They waved back when we asked if they could hear us. We repeated our message, "To climb the cliff and to walk north toward the friendly Marines." Soon the young girls started to climb the cliff followed by their parents and others. Suddenly five soldiers emerged from the cave mouth and were lined up. Then an Officer came out of the cave and put a bullet in each head. Their bodies slid down to the crashing surf trailing blood all the way down.

Then one young girl who had started to climb the slope of the cliff began to return to the cliff edge, sat down and combed her long black hair. With hair tidy, she stood up and jumped off the cliff into the pounding waves. She had greater fear of Americans than she had of death. This was a sad and tragic loss of a young girl who didn't live long enough to learn the truth. Those climbing the cliff slope never looked back. We were pleased they were listening and moving toward safety.

On the cliff one family man with a wife and two children dressed in little red outfits just sat and stared at the sea stoically. Then the father rose picked up one child and hurled that child over the cliff into the surf breaking on the rocks. He hesitated for a minute and the picked up the second child and repeated his act. Then taking his wife's hand, he helped her up and holding hands they walked off the cliff together.

We maneuvered closer to waters edge of the cliff. What we had thought were varied colored rocks awashed by the sea were human bodies clothed in bright colored garments in very grotesque positions. Nearby other people were bathing in shallow pools and appearing not to be disturbed by the mangled bodies awash at the cliff's end.

A crewmember called our attention to a group of possibly 30 soldiers who were walking and running for the slope climbing to the top of the cliff. From the cave mouth came the crack of rifle shots and several runners dropped in their strides on the slope. Several others jumped into the sea and started to swim toward us. One made it. He was sixteen years old and after being pulled aboard he said, "He did not want to die so young." Shortly after sun down we broadcast our final message that we would return tomorrow.

Dawn came peacefully on the 5th of August and we were pleased to hear that over 1,000 of the Tinian population had come to our stockade. Back on the cliff area we observed the groups as we had seen on the day before. Some were walking up the slope toward the north and then we spotted 6 or 7 Japanese soldiers behind a large rock. They had grenades in their hands and rifles slung over one shoulder. We could see the Marines merging from different areas and with our loud speakers we call out to them, "Marines on the cliff. There are seven enemy soldiers with grenades and rifles behind the big rock you are approaching." To the Japanese we said," Obey our commands and walk out with your hands up. The Marines will not shoot." The Japs remained still and when the Marines were just about a throwing distance the Japs stood up to throw the grenades. They never got the grenades in the air as the Marines rifles cracked and they fell where they stood.

We shifted our view to the left and to our utter amazement and horror we witnessed a no end procession of people throwing their children off the cliff and then jumping after them. The surf pounded against the cliff's base rocks which was now covered with broken and tangled bodies. On the slope above there was also a steady procession going north.

We were directed to stay in the area after we picked up two swimmers about noontime. They were exhausted and deeply frightened and begged us not to kill them. We patrolled the coast continuing our broadcasting, " Walk to the north for a safe haven. Many of your friends are already there.'" At sunset we made progress toward the harbor ending our two days of broadcasting to save lives. Upon arrival we learned that nearly 4,000 people poured into the stockade. Later we talked with one man in the stockade. He said, " He couldn't understand why we were trying to save their lives when they were our enemy? Why did you go to so much trouble?"

Source: Article by Lt Cliff Graham in Coronet Magazine, dated 06-01-1945. All credit goes to Lt Graham's article which is repeated here so later generations of American and Japanese will know what occurred.

M/Sgt Klabo is Recognized

The progress in learning to fly the B-29s brought recognition to the flight crew of the airplane, however those who performed the maintenance duties were often sadly overlooked. The article sent to me by Andy Nazario entitled "Warbird History," B-29 Super Fortress, by Pilot Charles G. Chauncey, introduces another B-29 aircraft named "**Goin' Jessie**" and worthy of note in this book.

In July 1945 the "**Goin' Jessie**" a new B-29, was now making its combat home on Tinian Island. The B 29 bombing flights from Tinian to Japan were 24 hours per day and seven days per week. According to Chauncey, when the war ended little did we realize that the "**Goin' Jessie**" had completed 50 missions without a single abortion. Said another way it simply means never did the crew have to return to the base without completing the mission because of mechanical troubles. Not once did "**Goin' Jessie**" fail to be airborne with the super ton loads of explosives being carried to the enemy's shores. On the southern end of Tinian Island was the "Bone Yard" where the B-29s that had crashed on take-off were piled. Because of the good ground crew's maintenance the "**Goin' Jessie**" never had a mishap and all flight crewmembers made it safely home.

Another outstanding record achieved by "**Goin' Jessie**" occurred on 10 July 1945, at 0118 hours while over Wakayama, Japan. It was computed that if all the tons of bombs dropped on the enemy Axis of Germany, Italy and Japan were added up, it was on this flight that the "**Goin' Jessie**" was credited with the dropping of the 2 millionth ton of bombs on the Axis since the beginning World War II. The date, tonnage and time of the bombing were confirmed by Squadron Commander Colonel Luschen.

Chauncey's article went on to say, "We believed we had

a good flight crew, a good aircraft and an excellent ground crew led by Master Sergeant Einar S. Klabo." The Master Sergeant preferred to be called "Curley." Reviewing "**Goin' Jessie's**" records showed 808 combat hours, or 135,000 miles, or five and one half times around the world, and had specifically dropped 645,000 pounds of explosives on Japanese targets.

In order to accomplish this record it required 12 replacement engines, three sets of tires, 295,000 gallons of gasoline, and more than 5,000 gallons of oil. Flight crews were readily recognized for their outstanding performances but the ground crews who maintained those successful aircrafts were often overlooked.

Because M/Sgt Klabo's outstanding performance kept the "**Goin' Jessie**" going for the entire record setting 50 successful missions, Pilot Chauncey felt something special should be done recognizing him.

Fortunately, at a luncheon at the Tinian "Officer's Club," Chauncey was seated next to General Carl Spaatz who asked if he could help with any problem. Chauncey related the problem of getting recognition for the fine maintenance work of M/Sgt Klabo. General Spaatz hearing the full story on M/Sgt concurred and later in the afternoon presented Klabo with the Legion of Merit medal.

Post Script: This story is included in this book to bring recognition to the many other B-29 pilots and maintenance crews who were soon overlooked when the flight of the Enola Gay by Colonel Paul Tibbetts introduced the "Atomic Bombs"

Colonel Tibbetts' flight was outstanding in that no one knew what the after effects would be on the aircraft after the bomb was dropped. The scientists felt the mushroom cloud could have a deleterious effect on the delivery aircraft and the escape from the cloud was of great concern.

Colonel Tibbetts and his crew were aware of the risks involved but did not hesitate to proceed with the dangerous assignment believing it would end the war quickly.

If for some reason the Atomic Bomb wasn't achieved the other B-29 flight and maintenance crews would continue to labor bringing the war to the Japanese homeland. They too were always at risk because of the heavy bomb loads, the long distant flights, and the Japanese Zero attacks. By including the **"Goin' Jesse"** story World War II is revisited to honor the maintenance crews.

The 509th Air Group
B-29 Base on Tinian Island

Just outside the Officer's Club on Tinian Island, a Navy SeaBee Officer overheard a senior Command Officer's comment regarding the *USS Indianapolis* brief anchorage off Tinian Island in late July 1945. The ranking Officer thought it strange that the *USS Indianapolis*, a heavy cruiser, was acting like a Navy transport. As soon as the large boxes were unloaded the *USS Indianapolis* weighed anchor and departed. The SeaBee Officer moved closer to the speaking Officer saying, "Excuse me Sir, were those boxes, by any chance consigned to the 509th Air Group?" The answer came back, "Why yes, they were. How did you know that?" The SeaBee Officer responded, "I didn't. I was just guessing." This was one of the many strange things occurring since the 509th Air Group arrived on Tinian Island.

A few days later the local mimeographed newspaper circulated on the Island carried the headline–"General Spaatz Decorates Colonel Paul Tibbetts At North Field." Colonel Tibbetts was the commanding Officer of the 509th Air Group and was the recipient of the Distinguished Service Cross for a special mission over the Japanese Empire.

The article continued that General Carl "Tooey" Spaatz, Commander of the Strategic Air Force, had made a special trip to Tinian to bestow the medal on Colonel Paul Tibbetts.

Well, speaking about dropping a bomb on morale, this really made some of the flight crews of the 313th Air Group with 15 or more flights over Japan, do some rapid calculating. If one flight over Japan can get you the DSC, where will General Spaatz get enough medals to cover the rest of the crews and Officers who have been doing this every night for several months?

The 509th Air Group was a newly arrived Air Group and had kept to themselves since their arrival. Anytime they were questioned as to their mission they responded, "We came here to end the war!" It was a braggadocios response that invoked a lot of irritation from those who for many months were making these flights nightly. The 509th were the newcomers. The new kids on the block and pretty cocky at that. Their group was also composed many high ranking Officers and a group of civilians who appeared to be "non-flying Officers.

As a new group to the island, they had not seen the B-29 graveyard at the end of Tinian Island on Broadway road. They had not felt the emotional drain when a B-29 crashed on take off losing the aircraft and its crew. The 509th just had not been on Tinian long enough to see and feel these things. It was just not a case of coming to Tinian to make a few bombing runs and then the war would be over. The 313th heavy bomb ladened Air Group faced that risk on every take off.

Those with less irritation felt there had to be more to the awarding of the DSC and were willing to wait for more details to surface. Certainly the 509th offered a positive attitude toward the common sought goal. All B-29 crews wanted the defeat of Japan and an ending of the war. The rumored invasion of Japan was schedule for late October or early November. Now in July this was three months away and many more B-29 night bombing missions would be initiated from Tinian. Night flights are of course, followed by the daytime B-29 reconnaissance flights to evaluate the results of the night flights and then to plan for the next nights bomb targets. Rumors spiraled upward and irritations soared with the publication of the local newspaper called "The 313th Wing Talk." Then four hours later the local Tinian radio station interrupted the musical program for a special statement.

"President Harry Truman has just announced that the Japanese City of Hiroshima was destroyed today by a single atomic bomb. This new bomb is more powerful than 20,000 tons of TNT."

Source: Condensed article by "The 313th Wing Talk" by Jacob A. Evan published by the *American Weekly* on 08-14-1960. The *American Weekly* is no longer in business, per Library sources.

Three days later the second atomic bomb was dropped on Nagasaki. Five days later the Japanese agreed to the unconditional surrender terms on August 14, 1945. The old expression of "victory" when said in Latin reads as follows–**VENI—VIDE—VICI—**. (They came, they saw, they conquered.) The 509th had it right and when they said, —
"They came to end the war and they did!"

L. Peter Wren

Bruno Shuster's Secret

The following is a letter from Walter Shuster of Shelton, Ct. who writes regarding his brother Crew Chief Bruno Shuster's wartime experiences with the B-29s on Tinian Island. I had asked Walter to relate what his brother told him about the Tinian Air Base and the B-29 flights. Here is his answer.

18 July 2001

Dear Peter:

The *USS Indianapolis* had just left the "A Bomb" at Tinian where my brother, Bruno Shuster, was a B-29 Crew Chief. He saw the Enola Gay at night all lit up and surrounded by lots of Military Police while the bomb was being loaded on the Enola Gay.

Now in the Navy a 4.0 score is perfect. In the Airforce a grade of "ZERO" was a perfect score. My brother had a record of 38 successful launches with "Zero" aborted flights. Under his supervision, his crew repaired and inspected B-29s before being pronounced ready for loading and the next bombing mission. This was so unusual that one of the Generals asked Bruno Shuster how was he managing to accomplish this feat.

Bruno gave him the standard operational procedure (SOP) which the General didn't accept. The General had heard that on take off every crewmember prayed their engines would not sputter and the overloaded plane would clear the field. Further Crew Chief Bruno reported he remained on board the B-29 during those hours for each overhaul test. If after those 24-hour repairs and tests went well, he felt the plane was safe and ready for flight. He then could catch a little sleep.

Well, the General carefully listened to all this but still believed there was something not being said. Bruno was so self-assured that his flights would clear the field, that the General just knew there had to be more to it. With the General now boring in and almost threatening hard times for Crew Chief Bruno, the secret ingredient was finally explained.

Bruno admitted to the General that he was using the Pilots monthly allotment of liquor to bribe the Parts Crib attendant in order to get "new" spark plugs. Bruno had found that even after sandblasting the used plugs, there still remained a burned sediment resting on the inside gap which could be a possible cause of failure. Used plugs just didn't last very long. I can assure you that the Enola Gay took off with brand new spark plugs, as Crew Chief Bruno Shuster would have it no other way.

/s/ Walter J. Shuster

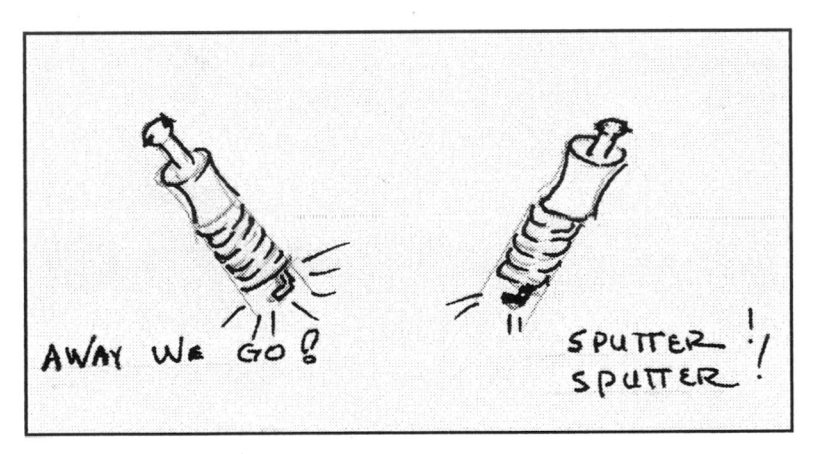

If spark plugs could speak

Chapter Six
Battles near Japan

The *USS Franklin* (CV 13) in Poetic Form
Inspired by 18-Year-Old Mate John H. Furrow

A Sea Bee on Okinawa Island
Captain James R. Mims CEC USNR

The Kamikaze Who Survived
As told by 18-Year-Old Mate Marland Moreau

A Flag Raising Witnessed
As told by 18-Year-Old Mate Tom Mumford

The *USS Franklin* (CV 13) in Poetic Form
Inspired by 18-Year-Old Mate John H. Furrow

This story comes to me from a Richmond, Virginian named Joseph Patterson and his newly found friend, John H. Furrow of Roanoke Virginia. Joe Patterson lost his brother, James Francis Patterson, Jr. who was a member of the crew on the *USS Franklin*. James F. Patterson's remains were never recovered and he is listed as "lost at sea."

John Furrow was an 18-year-old survivor of the *USS Franklin* and a watertender striker with an assigned station in the *USS Franklin's* boiler room. Joe and John met in 2004 at the Ship's 60th Reunion with each searching for a shipmate who was then aboard the *USS Franklin* in 1944. Fortune smiled on Joe Patterson because he found his brother James' son at the reunion seeking information on his dad, James Francis Patterson (lost at sea).

Joe called to tell me how glad he was to have finally located his nephew and to set up an interview with the survivor, John Furrow so this story could be included in this book. Much has been written on the *USS Franklin* (CV 13) so I decided to tell the story as follows.

The *USS FRANKLIN* (CV 13)
(The Ship that wouldn't sink)

The USS Carrier "Big Ben" has been
Written up often, and time and time again
But there is a story that has yet to be told
About the sailor just out of boot camp and 18-years-old.

In engineering spaces his assigned watch, he stood
Operating is the boiler and he is learning all he could
He noted one ladder down and one ladder up and out
Where escape would be slow, if in a hurry and wanted out

The morning GQ was over and the air launch was called
For flying aircraft to unload the bombs they hauled
The Big Ben steamed full speed off the Okinawa shore
This operation was destined to blast open a door

For Marines and Army to storm the beach
To defeat all the enemy within their reach
Then the CB's would come and build another airfield
From which our bombs, the enemy would violently reel

This is today's operation, but to Big Ben's dismay
A kamikaze bomber destroys the well-planned day
For it slipped through the defense and skips a large
    bomb
Across Big Ben's deck now with aircraft fully armed

Gasoline tanks ignite, bombs explode and a fire does
    rage
Trained crews with fire hose, the fire they engage
Airmen on the flight deck are blown over the side
The many wounded, and burned, now swim in the
    morning tide

Below the boiler room quickly fills with acrid smoke
Wet cloths cover noses, eyes smart, some men choke
And all hands listen for the command they fearfully
    dread
But the command to "Abandon Ship" is never said

The engineering rooms are in the belly of the ship
All hands stand steady, their courage doesn't dip
Then the senior mate directs the 18-year-old
"To climb up the ladder and report what you behold."

He is selected to go because he is small and nimble
His body will slip thru the hatch as neat as a thimble
Then back down he comes to his assigned station
Reporting his sights and his frightening observation

The heat is intense, the smoke and lack of ventilation
Requires fresh air, or this will be their expiration
The 18-year-old searches for assurance from his senior
　mate
As he stands his watch, knowing well what could be their
　fate

Tho' ship is damaged and tilted toward an awkward
　plane
The Captain takes action so the pilots can fly again
When the Cruiser, USS Santa Fe with seaman's skill and
　pride
Comes in close to rescue airmen, with a high line trol-
　ley ride

And the Destroyers of "Des-Ron Fifty Eight Point Two"
Rescue the men blown over board from the ocean blue
Then the "Oil King" speaks from the bottom where the
　ship was first built
Saying," Captain, with your permission I can reduce the
　ship's tilt!"

The deck fires roar and the ship unfortunately slowly
　drifts
Toward the near Japanese Island, there in the mist
Then USS Pittsburgh is called to take Big Ben in tow
Connections are made, but the towing is painfully slow

Engines are restarted in spaces below, on deck they release the tow
The Captain commands "Steer leeward of the winds
that blow"
The flight deck fire subsides and that battle is won
The engines gain speed and out of enemy range, they
run

From the depths of the ship, the deceased are being
recovered
Ship mates and the Chaplain search, their identity to
discover
The 18-year-olds duty relieved, are now with funeral rites
tending
And they join in the final prayers the Chaplain is sending

The burials continue steady through morning, noon
and night
The Chaplain reads from his book on the final funeral
rite
The American flag covers the body before being released
to the sea
The flag is recovered for the Chaplain's next matc's final plea

Each day with condolence the Captain pens a word of
sorrow
To the deceased sailor's family who will sadly learn to-
morrow
On how their loved one served and how the Big Ben
Was a winner because of dedicated men like him.

The Big Ben moves across the Pacific, with a small crew
To see Pearl Harbor come finally into view
Underway again though listing to the right, but still water
    tight
She passes through the Canal on her homeward plight

Then New Yorkers standing on the East River Bank
Send shouts of joy for the ship that could not be sank
Now this 18-year-old sailor who had faced the perils of
    the sea
Has arrived home safely, and is as thankful as one can
    be.

So ends these verses speaking of the Carrier, Big Ben
And we pray no other ship will suffer like this again.
But if there should ever be such a disaster on the seas
We know there will be brave men again, such as these.

By L. Peter Wren,
LCDR USNR (ret) (01-16-'05)

Notes of Explanation:

A **trolley block** rides on a high line stretched between
two ships. The block has a hook below the trolley which
can carry a seat, stretcher or a cargo net. This is the method
to transfer men, Doctors, wounded or supplies while underway at sea.

Oil King is a petty officer in the Engineering Division
who transfers by pumps the fuel or water in storage to keep
the ship level in the water. This is a full time duty as the ship
continues to burn oil and use water for cooking, drinking,
& washing.

The tow occurred when the Big Ben drifted just 38 miles from the smallest Japanese Island Shikoku. American forces did not want the ship captured with the Captain and crew on board. The Japanese military reported Big Ben sunk.

Task Force 58 The *USS Franklin* was of the Essex class Carriers and was assigned to the above task force with other Carriers, Battleships, Cruisers, and Destroyers. In addition a Naval Air group was housed aboard as the Naval Air Arm.

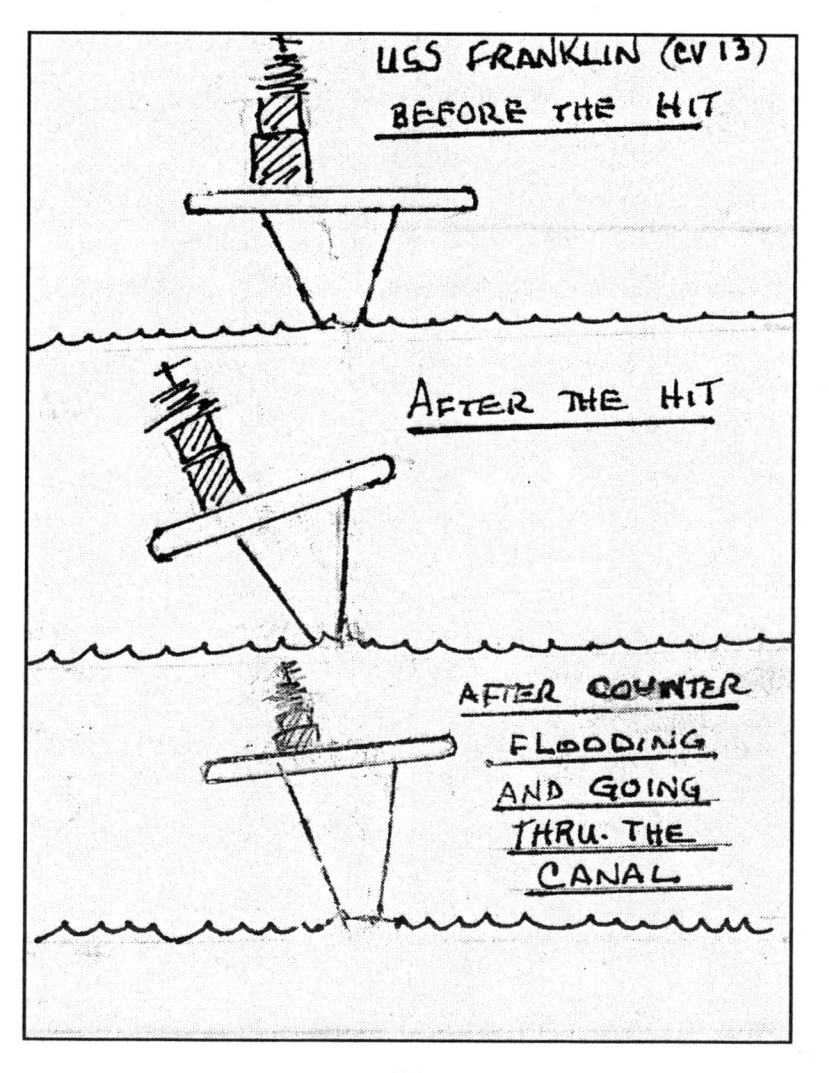

Engineering Spaces are comprised of the Boiler rooms which make steam for propulsion and generating electrical power. Boilers also provide the water for cooking, washing, drinking and laundry services. The Engine rooms use the steam to control the speed of the ship and other necessary functions to make the ship a fighting platform while at sea. On all ships there are service tanks and storage tanks. As fuel and gasoline are pumped from the service tanks to run the ship and fuel the airplanes, the Oil King pumps from the storage tanks into the service tanks to keep the ship as a level platform. When the ship gets low on the combustibles the Oil King will flood the storage tanks with seawater to maintain the level position. The Big Ben had ruptured tanks causing the tilt of the flight deck. The Oil King did what he could to lessen the tilt.

The 18-year-olds are now in their seventies and soon will be passing. These verses are written to help another generation learn what was demanded of 18 year olds during WW II serving on a ship in March 1945.

L. Peter Wren

A Sea Bee on Okinawa Island
Captain James R. Mims CEC USNR

With the securing of Iwo Jima the leaders of the Armed Forces held a strategy conference. Okinawa was just 340 miles from the Japanese Homeland. There were three airfields in operation on Okinawa which would provide easy take-offs for bombing the Japanese Inland Sea which carried most of their war traffic. Also these three airfields would make easy bombing flights on the traffic moving in the Yellow Sea and down the China coast to Taiwan and further south, where the war effort was still ensuing in Maylaysia. The Philippine Islands were not fully secured and a base in Taiwan was needed to cut off the replenishment of Japanese China-Burma forces.

Lt. Colonel A. J. Barker, in his book *Okinawa*, relates the vision of the different commands. General Mac Arthur wanted the next thrust made into the large Island of Luzon in the Philippines. Admiral King wanted the next thrust be applied to the Island of Taiwan which was now fully Japanese held and sheltering and supplying war materials for transit down the east coast of China. Admiral Spruance wanted the invasion of Okinawa because of its nearness to the Japanese mainland. His view was to by-pass the Philippines and Taiwan Islands just like was done in earlier operations. Admiral Nimitz was able to work out a compromise between the planners and it was decided MacArthur would take about half of his troops to Luzon. On April 1, 1945 the other half of the Army, lead by Lieutenant General Simon Bolivar Buckner would join Admiral Spruance amphibious force and Marine Corps Lt. General Geiger 's Marines in the attack on Okinawa.

Meanwhile the Japanese high commands estimated the next American thrust would be on Okinawa. Because the Japanese fleet was decimated in the Battle of the Philip-

136

pine Sea (also known as the MarianasTurkey Shoot) the concept of the Kamikaze attacks would dominate their defense. The Allied invasion of Okinawa was called "Operation Iceberg."

In late March 1945 a heavy bombardment by the American battleships and cruisers preceded the invading troops Okinawa landing on April 1, 1945. The Japanese issued a Kamikaze plan known as "TenGo." This amounted to ten large groups of kamikaze planes attacking American Forces from April 6th, 1945 until June 22, 1945. It was in this early shore bombardment (March 1945) that the *USS Indianapolis* was struck by a kamikaze plane and was eventually returned to the West Coast Shipyards for repair. The Carrier, *USS Franklin* was also a war casualty in the Okinawa invasion and returned to the United States under its own power. The *USS Indy* returned to the Pacific Theater with special orders from now President Harry Truman, to proceed with all speed to Tinian Island with a special cargo now on board. (Hiroshima Bomb)

Also in the "Operation Iceberg" was the return of a reconstituted British Pacific Fleet to be meshed with the American fleet off Okinawa serving with distinction against Okinawa and Japan.

The amphibious forces put the Army, Marines, and CB's ashore on April 1, and each group followed its action plan. The Marines swept north of the Island, the CB's headed for the airfields to prepare them for the B-29 bombers, and Lt General Buckners 10th Army swept south toward Naha. The Marine found light resistance as they moved north as a large part of the people occupying the land were anti-Japanese. The Chinese and Ainu natives welcomed the Americans and helped them dispose of the Japanese who held them as slaves. The Marines stationed enough troops to secure the northern part of the island and returned south to aid Buckner's Tenth Army.

Captain James R. Mims (CEC) USNR of Richmond Va. was then a Senior Lieutenant with one of the many Construction Battalions on Okinawa. In our conversation, Mims spoke of the events he vividly recalls. First is the loss of Lt General Simon B. Buckner, USA. On June 18th he learned that General Buckner went up to an observation post to oversee an enemy position. In that short move to see better, the observation post was struck by mortar fire and the shells caused a large block of coral to mortally wound him. He died in minutes after being hit. Captain Mims said it was tragic indeed as he died within two miles of his goal and just four days before the Island was deemed secured. Mims said he had an urgent call to bring a master painter, a gallon of gray paint and a good service paintbrush immediately to Buckner's Command site. The army had quickly built a wooden coffin in which Lt. General Buckner lay, and they wanted it painted gray before the burial ceremony began. Mims' painter completed the assignment. Unfortunately Mims was called away to another project and was unable to witness the ceremonial burial honors rendered in behalf of Lt.General Buckner. Shortly after the ceremony the local command suggested that they rename the bay of water over which his gravesite looked. To this day Nakagusuka Bay is now known officially as Buckner Bay. Another site that held Mims attention was a Christian church tower which was used as a Japanese sniper position controlling a valley. The basic church was repeatedly struck by mortars and large gunfire. Most every part of the structure was riddled and wracked by explosives. Yet the spire of the church carrying a Christian cross remained intact. When the area was finally captured, the dead Japanese warriors lay all around. Captain Mims said the presence of that cross on the tower created an aura of peace. Death and destruction were everywhere but a sense of peace permeated that scene.

Source: Oral history by Captain JamesR.Mims, CEC USNR, of Richmond, Va.
American Naval History by Jack Sweetman, 1984
Okinawa, by LtCol A. J. Barker,1981

Japanese snippers were located in the above Christian Church during the battle for Okinawa. Captain James Mims, CEC, USNR said with all the havoc of war the cross on the steeple remained intact.

L. Peter Wren

The Kamikaze Who Survived
As told by 18-Year-Old Mate Marland Moreau

It will seem strange to the reader that this book will cover two Japanese Nationals who were once hated and now are respected because World War Two brought our nations together. These Japanese Nationals have taken outstanding personal action to help bind the American and Japanese relationships. They are worth revealing to all Americans and to all Nations in the future so that all will understand that America will fight to win, and will assist any country in its needs and will never come to occupy.

Most of this information is from Marland Moreau of Flint, Michigan in answer to my request to peruse the material he possessed on the *USS Callaghan* (DD-792) on Lieutenant (jg) Kaoru Hasegawa, I J N (Imperial Japanese Navy). In October 2004 while attending the *USS Callaghan* Reunion, I met with Marland and Lt Bucetti who relived and recited the story again.

This is the story of Kaoru Hasegawa , a Japanese citizen, who graduated as a pilot from the Imperial Japanese Naval Academy in March of 1944. After graduation he received some advanced training and taught as an officer at the USA Air Group and several other Groups. In February of 1945 he was stationed at Kisarazu Air Base as a crewmember of a twin-engined "Ginga" bomber. {*Ginga means galaxy. This is the twin-engined bomber which the Americans named "Francis" for recognition purposes*}

In March and April Hasegawa under went intensive training at Matsushima. On May 21,1945 he received orders to form and organize a Special Attack Force. {a.k.a. Kamikaze}. This was composed of thirty-six men divided into four elements with three bombers in each group On

140

25 May 1945, after four days of waiting for an assignment, the Senior Officers of the school, delivered to each crew-member a "*makunouchi bento*," or a variety box lunch which is a first class meal given under the special circumstances. It consisted of a large omelette, boiled and flavored meat with vegetables, and a scoop of white rice capped with a pickled red plum. (*The red plum represents the rising sun which is the emblem on the National flag of Japan.*) Slowly savoring this bento, Kasegawa realized that he would die before this rice became part of his flesh and blood. He bitterly laughed at himself as he wound his watch out of habit before boarding his bomber. He realized his watch only needed to run until a little after ten forty on the 25th of May 1945.

Hasegawa was not afraid of dying. He just felt a profound loneliness. He would no longer see his good friends nor be able to see his father, mother and brothers. This would be the last time he would see Japan's beautiful mountains and rivers. These thoughts made him feel very lonesome. However, if he could help the people of his country more by dying, then there would be no greater sacrifice. Wholeheartedly he believed that.

At five o'clock on that May morning, the Japanese Navy Special Attack Corps {*Kamikaze*} took off from Air Base #2 in Miho Shimane. Their target was the US Fleet in the sea off Okinawa. All bombers would directly attack the ships which were centered around an Aircraft Carrier which they had been tracking. As a Lieutenant junior grade he was in command of this 12-bomber operation.

Their plan called for each of the four elements to break from the formation and approach the target from different directions. The leading three bombers were supposed to swing around west of Oshima Island and attack South and Southeast.

As they passed off Kyushu, with Tanega Shima Island on their right, it started to rain in torrents. With the rain cloud hanging so low on the sea surface, the poor visibility forced them to fly extremely low; only fifty to one hundred meters above the sea. Water dripped from the windshield. The humidity and high temperatures in his aircraft were unbearable. So Hasegawa undid his helmet chinstrap and took off the safety belt around his waist without the slightest thought that this would later save his life.

His bomber had a crew of three: Hasegawa, the pilot in the nose, behind him were Warrant Officer (Koyama) and Petty Officer (Yoshida). Except for a few exchanges of commands and reports through the speaking tube, all three remained silent concentrating on their progress. Unfortunately one of bombers of their group was forced to turn back because of a faulty engine. They expected to arrive in the vicinity of the enemy at ten-forty in the morning. However, they could see nothing at ten-thirty or even at ten-forty. They were surrounded by a milkly white cloud, and Hasegawa began to feel very frustrated.

At ten forty-two, however, his field of vision suddenly opened. Immediately he could see up to five to six miles ahead. Within his grasp were the enemies gray warships all lined up. He could see a huge ship, probably a Battleship surrounded by five or six Destroyers. {*This was the USS West Virginia and surrounded by its escorts one of which is the USS Callaghan DD 792*}

Since his aircraft flew below the low hanging clouds, and just above sea, the enemy's radar did not detect them. He looked immediately for the aircraft carrier. (*USS Franklin*). Naturally if he were going to crash, he should crash into the carrier as that was the mission of the Special Attack Corps {Kamikaze}.

At that moment the enemy fleet began to fire on them. For a moment he ducked back into the clouds without finding the carrier. However, he guessed the Carrier must be behind the fleet. He turned left in the cloud and headed for the enemy's rear. Again he broke out of the clouds and Hasegawa signaled a "bank" by rocking his wings from left to right, which was the sign for the other bomber to break off. He banked slowly several times permitting the lone accompanying bomber to distance itself.

As soon as he signaled the bomber following him, his aircraft was surrounded by a fierce barrage of gunfire. Hasegawa saw countless geysers of water on the sea. {*A standard procedure for the American ship's guns, was to direct fire power at the low flying aircraft as well as to shoot at the sea in front of the aircraft causing water geysers. If the aircraft's propeller struck the geyser of water it would cause the aircraft to tumble or cartwheel into the sea*}. Hasegawa turned further left trying to get to the rear of the fleet. At that moment, he felt a great shock and seven or eight bullets penetrated his bomber. He called the crew by name through the speaking tube, "Koyama" and there was no answer. He screamed, "Yoshida!" then he felt his airplane roll to the left, falling into the sea. His memory stopped there.

As he gained consciousness he felt himself in the sea and saw his copilot also clinging to the floating aircraft wing from his plane. {*Remember, earlier he had loosened his helmet and disconnected his life jacket strap. Now the airplane wing is keeping both afloat*}. The *Callaghan* was close by and since all Kamikaze in that attack group were shot down, CDR Charles Bertholf, skipper of the *USS Callaghan*, ordered a motor whale boat launched to recover Hasegawa and his copilot. {Geneva Convention rules do not permit anyone, friend or foe to be left in the open sea if a rescue can be accomplished.}

The next time Hasegawa regained consciousness, he heard coarse English being spoken {probably cursing his Nationality} and he recognized that he was aboard a ship. A medical corpsman was bending over him taking his blood pressure. "Damn," he thought, "I am not supposed to be alive!" He had difficulty in breathing and couldn't move his right leg. Hasegawa asked if they had saved the other two crewmembers. A sailor assisting in the medical area answered that they just had the one other man who was holding on to the floating wing. {Note—The reader of this story may wonder how Hasegawa spoke and understood English. English had become the second language in the Imperial Naval Academy training. All students were required every Saturday morning to watch an American movies for three hours. Watching American movies was to improve their speech patterns and to increase their vocabularies}.

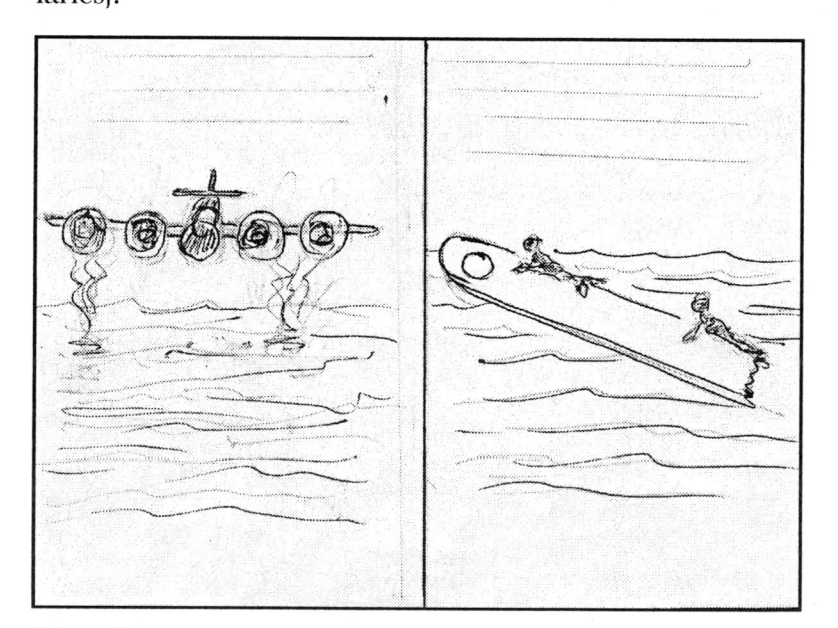

Kkamikaze hits water geysers and cartwheels into the sea.

Japanese crewmembers hang on to floating wing and are rescued by the *USS Callaghan.*

Hasegawa was treated for his injuries and after ten hours in *Callaghan*'s sickbay he was transferred to the *USS New*

Mexico. Later he was transferred to the Naval Hospital in Guam and then to the hosptal in Hawaii for additional treatment. His copilot died on the *USS Callaghan.* Hasegawa spent 14 months as a prisoner of war and in the fall of 1946 he returned to his home in Ashiya, Japan. "It was devastated," he recalled. "All I could see was rubble!"

{*As a further note, the USS Callaghan experienced trials of her own. On July 29, 1945, just two months after Hasegawa aircraft had been shot down, the USS Callaghan was the victim of another Kamikaze attack. The Callaghan was due to be relieved by the USS Laws at 0130 hours on the 29th of July to return to the States for up grading. Unfortunately the Callaghan was struck and sunk loosing 46 of her crew and one officer at 0051 hours on that same date. This was 39 minutes before the Callaghan would be relieved to head for the States, and about 24 hours before the sinking of the USS Indianapolis which had brought the A-Bomb to the South Pacific. The relief ship, the USS Law, became a rescue ship as well as the replacement vessel. World War II ended 15 days later on 14 August 1945 with the surrender of Japan.*}

Up until May of 1995, {*This is 50 years since Hasegawa's mission against the American Fleet in the Sea off Okinawa*} Hasegawa had not spoken to anyone about the incident or his rescue. Because his bomber accidentally tumbled into the sea, he was the only one of his crew remaining alive. Kamikaze pilots are not supposed to live. Morcover he spent 14 months as a prisoner of war, which was very dishonorable in those days. For a long time he felt he should remain silent. But with assistance from an Imperial Naval Academy officer he was able to contact a retired US Naval Officer who helped him get the information on the *USS Callaghan* and its reunion. After contacting one of the crewmembers who was aboard at the time of his rescue, he was invited to join the *USS Callaghan's* Reunion in Pigeon Forge, Tennessee.

Here he met crewmembers who were able to fill in the

gaps of his memory during those hours after he was shot down. While at the reunion Hasewaga casually mentioned how foolish he felt winding his watch the morning of the kamikaze mission. At that moment, LT Buccetti who was the Executive officer on the USS *Callaghan*, handed Hasegawa his watch saying, "Would you like to wind it again?" Further he received the wallet of his co-pilot who had died aboard the USS *Callaghan*, and it still contained the co-pilot's family pictures.

Since the war Hasegawa has become Chairman of the Rengo Company, a large manufacturer of paper products throughout Asia. In gratitude for the Callaghan's crew who welcomed him to their reunion and for filling in the information he lacked, he donated $10,000 to the US Navy Memorial Fund. On 31 July 1995 Hasegawa assisted in placing a wreath at the Naval Memorial in Washington, DC. During this ceremony Hasegawa met Naval Memorial Chairman, Admiral Elmo Zumwalt, who was highly impressed with this former enemy. According to the report Admiral Zumwalt suggested that the goodwill Hasagawa generated be passed on down to a new generation of Americans and Japanese. Zumwalt's suggestion was readily received and the U.S.–Japanese Maritime Youth Exchange Program was instituted. The U.S. Navy Memorial Foundation of the Navy Institute now plays an active roll. Since 1998, there has been an annual exchange of American and Japanese students participating in this youth program.

MORE NAVAL BACKGROUND ADDED

According to a recent encyclopedia on the history of the Showa Era (1926-1989) 3,535 Japanese military personnel died in the suicide attacks by the end of the war. United States records show that 16 naval vessels including the *Callaghan* were sunk and that 185 were damaged.

The *USS Indianapolis* (CA 35) was struck by a kamikaze in the March 1945 Okinawa operation and returned to the States for repairs and up-dating. The *USS Indianapolis* repaired and carrying some special equipment departed San Francisco on July 16, 1945 setting a speed record crossing the Pacific to Tinian Island. The "Cargo" being transported to Tinian was totally unknown to the ship's company and arrived on 26 July 1945. The Enola Gay, a B-29 American bomber, with Colonel Paul Tibbetts in command, would release that "special cargo" over Hiroshima, Japan on August 6, 1945. The world was now introduced to "Atomic Power." Meanwhile the *USS Indianapolis* en route to Leyte Gulf to rejoin the Pacific Fleet, was sunk by a enemy submarine. Due to a break down in communications the *USS Indianapolis* crew floundered on the sea for five days before the ship was known sunk. With a crew of 1197 only 317 survived. The narrator of this book was part of the rescue operation.

The 1945 listing of July sinkings are given here.
USS Underhill DE 682 sunk by kaiten 07-24-'45
USS Callaghan DD 792 Sunk by Kamikazi 07-29-'45 at 0051
USS Indianapolis CA 35 Sunk by torpedoes 07-30-'45 at 0030

Mr. Kaoru Hasegawa has been a great inspiration to many Americans and it is with sadness he died January 9, 2004. His outstanding love and respect for America and Japanese youth is recorded here for posterity to know. He was and is an honored patriot who speaks through these pages.

Sources: Oral Histories from *USS Callaghan* crewmembers Marland Moreau and LT Buccetti when Hasegawa was rescued.
The Dailey Yomiuri, May 25, 1998

Philadelphia Inquirer, July 31, 1995
The Knoxville News-Sentinel, July 30, 1995
Post Bulletin, Rochester, Minn., Sept 26, 1997
A copy of a report entitled "Hasegawa's Bomber in the
Okinawa Operation
Naval History Magazine, Sept / Oct issue 1995

A Flag Raising Witnessed
As told by 18-Year-Old Mate Tom Mumford

Having enlisted into the US Navy at age 18, Tom found himself at age 19 as a trained radioman, a bombardier, a gunner and part of the crew of a (TBF) Avenger Torpedo Bomber. Near Christmas in 1944, Tom, with the pilot and another mate were destined as replacements for a crew lost in action in the Pacific theater of the war. Tom and his crewmates were welcomed aboard the *USS Bismark Sea* (CVE 95) in late December in 1944. The " CVE carrier" is a smaller type carrier because of the shorter flight deck but a very necessary ship to fleet operations. The *USS Bismark Sea* had just returned from the "Battle of Leyte Gulf" when Tom and his shipmates were signed on as flight crew. One month later, on January 9, 1945 and now with VC Squadron 86, Tom was enroute to Luzon Island of the Philippines for the invasion of Lingayen Gulf.

Our TBF was assigned to flying anti-submarine patrols across the Lingayen Gulf. Our assignment also included glided bomb runs, strafing attacks and the sinking of Japanese barges. We destroyed bridges to prevent the Japanese troops from escaping. Another target was the local churches. Firing rockets at the churches was a rather grim task but necessary because the Japanese used these facilities to store their ammunitions. We had no choice in these targets. Shortly after this operation, the *USS Bismark Sea* was ordered to assist in the battle at Iwo Jima.

Our first bombing run on Iwo Jima was February 16, 1945, three days before D-Day. Our objective was to soften the Japanese forces guarding this small volcanic Island. Iwo Jima was teardrop shaped with Mt Suribachi, an inactive volcano, on one end of the island. The bombing run was across the narrow section of the island at the base of Mt Suribachi. Our targets were the Japanese anti-aircraft positions and bunkers that needed clearing before the initial invasion date, scheduled for February 19, 1945. This island was important in the "March to Tokyo" as it lay about 700 miles from the southern most island of Kyushu, Japan. There were three airfields on the island of Iwo Jima. Two were complete and the other was still under construction. Since our B-29 bombers now were "fire bombing" Japan and had a 1500 mile return flight from Tokyo to Tinian, it was important to have a near landing field in case of an emergency. Also with Iwo Jima captured it would be an ideal location for forays on the Japanese Islands and provide air support for the eventual planned Japanese invasion. Iwo Jimo appeared to have little or no life, until we pulled out of a bombing run. As rear airplane gunner, I could see the enemy come out from their tunnels or under-ground fortress, firing their anti-aircraft guns in an attempt to knock us out of the skies. Later I learned the Japanese had built underground facilities several levels below the surface which included a source of fresh water and fresh air piped in, electrical power and with living and berthing spaces and a sewage system. It was estimated that a force of twenty two thousand of their elite troops were stationed on this island and they were very heavily armed.

On February 19, the Marines began their landing but their progress was slowed to a halt as they hit the beach. The soft black volcanic ash provided no protection as a foxhole. Plus the Japanese had planned a blistering crossfire by mortars and rifle fire on the landing beach. The Marines were pinned down at the waters edge and their hope for relief had to come from the large caliber guns of the ships laying off the Island. Also the Navy Air needed to bomb out the concrete pillboxes obscured from the Naval ship's guns. Our job was to guide bombs into the pillboxes and hope we could return to the USS *Bismark Sea* for more bombs without a mishap. The hail of bullets from Iwo fortifications was heavy.

On D-Day plus two (February 21,1945) we flew bombing missions against the treacherous Japanese fire power to aid the advancement of the our Marines. With persistance, the Marines of the 3rd, 4th and 5th Divisions, finally crossed the base of Mt Suribachi. This area, of one and a half miles, was the stretch of land between the two seas surrounding the island. The anti aircraft flak was unbelievably heavy. The Japanese took pre-cautionary measures not to reveal their gun positions. After we made our glide bomb runs, the Japanese would run out of their caves and fire at us with their anti-aircraft weapons. It was then as rear gunner, that I would bring my 30-caliber machine gun to bear on the enemy, now popping up from their gopher-like holes.

We were making bomb runs with a group of four TBF's (torpedo planes). As a result of the intense enemy fire power some of our planes would crash into the sea astern of our aircraft or would crash-land on the deck of the USS *Bismark Sea*. On one occasion we were scheduled to make a bomb run on our own as the three other TBF aircraft were severely damaged. As we approached the target island with our bomb load, we were recalled by the USS *Bismark Sea* because they felt the odds were against our survival. We safely returned to the carrier and were thankful the mission was cancelled. We returned to the "Ready Room" on the USS *Bismark Sea*, waiting a call for the next flight mission. Waiting there with us was a radioman from a TBF from the USS *Saratoga*. This was the old USS *Saratoga* commissioned in 1927 and is the bigger and faster fleet type carrier. The USS *Saratoga* was under attack and was so badly damaged that the Saratoga pilots had to find another carrier to land on or ditch in the sea. Suddenly the sound of our anti-aircrafts guns echoed throughout the hull of my ship. The USS *Bismark Sea* was under a kamikaze attack.

The kamikaze is small Japanese airplane filled with explosives and piloted by a Japanese youth who is committed to suicide. The Kamikaze airplanes has just have enough fuel to fly from their home base to hit the nearest largest American vessel that the pilot can find. Six of the Kamikaze were on a level run at the *USS Bismark Sea.* Four were shot down. The 5th one managed to hit the starboard quarter with some damage but the 6th one struck the after-elevator lift. This was the fatal blow to the *USS Bismark Sea.* Explosions followed from the torpedoes, bombs and ammunitions on deck and in storage. Raging fires raced to both ends of the ship. All communications were lost but somehow the word to "Prepare to abandon ship" was issued. Shipmates helped those who were wounded or injured. Most of the men on the hanger deck and the mess hall were killed immediately. My shipmates were abandoning ship. More explosions occurred and the ship's lights went out. The fire was furious and bulkheads were buckling. I grabbed my pistol and another waist-type life belt and raced to the ship's bow. For a moment I thought I'd go below to save my sentimental picture album and "tailor made" blues. However in view the fast sinking ship they became a secondary priority.

Jumping off the bow from the height of a flight deck is harrowing experience of its own. You must keep your feet together, put your arms across your chest, while pulling down your life jacket so when you hit the water at the fast speed of the fall, that your life jacket doesn't crack you in the chin and knock you out. You must hold your breathe until you can propel yourself to the surface.

When finally surfaced, I found myself in very cold water, a rough sea and waves varying between ten to twenty feet. Darkness had come over us and the only light was the reflected light of the burning and sinking *USS Bismark Sea.* My childhood experience in the waves of the beaches of the Atlantic Ocean gave me confidence that somehow I would be rescued. Near me in the water was a raft that was overloaded with sailors and with some hanging on to its sides struggling to stay afloat. I had on my May West life jacket and the life belt so I was riding high in the waves. I spotted a red light and decided I would swim to it rather than stay with the crowd on that raft. As I swam I suddenly found myself about to be run over by a ship. The red light was the "port side" running light. Next thing I knew I was lit up by a search light and a rope was tossed near me. From the ship came a voice calling me to grab the rope, which I did. I was rescued by the *USS Edmonds*, a Destroyer Escort and I was very happy to leave the cold sea to its natural inhibitors but sorry to loose the *USS Bismark Sea.*

The next morning had to be a Saturday as the breakfast menu was Navy beans. This is the traditional breakfast on Saturdays. Usually the Captain conducts his weekly inspections of the living compartments and the ships galley, if we are not in a war operation. A clean ship and a well-fed ship is a happy ship. However the happiness of my rescue changed to the sad experience of a burial-at-sea. In the early dawn light the Edmond's crew had recovered several of the *USS Bismark Sea* shipmates floating on the sea. They were wearing their life jackets and floating upright but had died sometime during the night. Others were trapped on the burning ship, some drowned , some were strafed in the water by the Japs gun fire and others were attacked by sharks. The *USS Bismark Sea*'s records showed a loss of 328 men.

At the funeral ceremony *the USS Edmond,* the ship's chaplain read a prayer. We all bowed our heads. The American Flag draped over the sewed canvases was retained when the encased deceased mates slid into the sea. The ship's bell tolled the hour. The deceased names were entered in the ship's log. The watch was set and the crew returned to the ensuing war. It was the best that could be done for those who had given their all.

On February 23, 1945 Tom and several others rescued by the *USS Edmonds* were transferred to a troop transport ship where there was more adequate berthing. On D-Day plus four the Marines aboard the transport vessel were loaded in the landing craft and continued their assault on the Iwo Jima beach. Not being part of the transports ship's company we were able to watch the invasion from the wings of the ships's bridge. We shared the ship's binoculars so each would have a close up view of the battle. This turned out to be the greatest experience of our lives. Here we were with ringside seats seeing the two flag raisings at the peak of Mt. Suribachi. The first was a small American flag mounted on a discarded piece of enemy pipe. Since the flag was too small to be seen adequately on that mountaintop, a request was sent throughout the ships present for a larger flag. A second flag was discovered and rushed to the mountaintop. The raising of the second flag was photographed by Joe Rosenthal and although it became famous, there was considerable controversy as to whether the flag raising was a staged photograph by Rosenthal. As the word went out from ship to ship by semaphore and signal light you could hear from the surrounding ships, shouts of joy between the gun salvos. We shared the binoculars, watching the battle and the "Old Glory" waving proudly on the pole atop Mt. Suribachi. What a glorious sight! Can you imagine our joy?

The Iwo Jima battle lasted through March 25, 1945 (34 days) with 22,000 Japanese killed taking this island. American forces lost 25,000 casualties leaving behind 7000 grave mounds with crosses and stars of David implanted. This is the only battle in the Pacific where the Americans suffered more losses including the wounded than the Japanese suffered.

Since we were crew from the sunken *USS Bismark Sea,*
we were transported back to Hawaii for further assignment.
Our pay records, and our sea bag of clothing were lost in
the sinking so we all traveled in the same clothes in which
we were rescued. In Hawaii we reestablished our personal
and pay records and received new uniforms. Being survivors of a sinking we were granted passage to the States and
the first ship heading for the States was a wooden British
vessel named *City of Paris.* The ship was manned by a Hindu
crew and in very poor condition. If you got down-wind of
it, you could smell it a mile before you boarded it. But it
was a trip to the States and home. We, the *USS Bismark* Sea
survivors, slept on wooden tables in the mess hall and were
fed bread with well cooked worms and other insects in the
loaves. We reflected how we had objected to those *USS
Bismark Sea* Saturday morning inspections with the beans &
cornbread breakfasts. Now we understood why the weekly
inspections were a well-established US Naval tradition
aboard ship. Having had a payday in Hawaii I used my cash
in the *City of Paris* store to buy some candy bars and canned
peaches. This became my diet during the trip to the States

The war ended on September 2, 1945 with Japanese
surrendering on the *USS Missouri* in Tokyo Bay My release
from military service came in October 1946. I counted my
blessings and thanked God for a safe return home. Now at
age twenty-one I was a better American because of my tour
of duty. The sacrifice of my deceased shipmates gave me
the luxury of living in a free country and always being proud
of being a citizen of the USA. Having served in the US
Navy, I felt that the experience helped me to grow into
manhood with humility and dignity. GOD BLESS
AMERICA

Thomas Mumford

Chapter Seven
Surrender and Occupation

Occupation Day
Stories by Lt Frank Heald, USNR

The Victory Table

Occupation Kure, Japan
Jack Paul's Memoirs

Hiroshima
Vernon Skordahl Rides Shot Gun

Prisoners of War Freed
Geo. R. Clark's Story

Sights and Sounds of War Torn Japan
Colonel Lewis I. Held, US Army

Being Welcomed
Ensign L. Peter Wren USNR

Occupation Day

Stories by Lt Frank Heald, USNR

The following are excerpts coming from a several-paged mimeographed letter written by Lt. Franklin Heald, USNR, who preferred to be called Frank. For a short time we were shipmates on the *USS Coates*, (DE 685) in the Atlantic. Frank was transferred to the light Cruiser *USS San Diego* (CL 83) operating in the Pacific. As I remember it, Frank had experience in newspaper work before entering Naval service. With this background he was assigned as Public Information Officer (PIO) on the *USS San Diego*.

We shared correspondence with a series of short letters but soon after his departure to the *USS San Diego*, I was transferred to the *USS Bassett* (APD 73) and it took a little time before our letter exchanges were re-established. It was in September 1945 that I received a five-paged mimeographed letter from Frank which spelled out details of the "Occupation Day" as well as the "Surrender Ceremony." President Harry Truman succeeded President Franklin D. Roosevelt after his death in May 1945. Since President Truman was from Missouri, he designated the *USS Missouri* as the ship on which the formal surrender would take place in Tokyo Bay. The date was set for September 02, 1945.

The mimeographed letter was well received and when I was finally released from Naval service in 1946 I saved it with my Navy papers. It has stayed safely hidden all this time. The pages had stories of great interest and I feel compelled to share them with my readers. Now it is 60 years since they were typed. I have lost contact with Frank but I believe he was from New Hampshire. The local newspaper in Manchester recently advised the Franklin Heald was associated with the University of New Hampshire and at age 89 had died in August 2003. I feel quite sure he would approve of my sharing his writings with my readers. Other information from other Officers is added to these pages as is appropriate to fill in the total picture of these events.

LT. Frank Heald USNR Advises:

The *USS San Diego* was the first large major warship to drop anchor in Tokyo Bay when the hostilities ended on August 14, 1945. Captain Mullen, Commanding Officer of the *USS San Diego*, was informed his ship would be the base from which all "Occupation Plans" would be coordinated. Lieutenant Heald's letter contains some interesting events which will nowhere appear in the formal surrendering of Japan. This first hand information of various activities which places the reader in a front seat of this historical event.

LT. Frank Heald Writes:

The Japanese had surrendered on August 14, 1945 and "Occupation Day" was set for August 30, 1945. This meant that the American and Allied Forces would be placing troops in Japan and on various Japanese controlled bases to accept their surrender (for example Truk Islands, Formosa, and Korea). Also it meant the freeing of American and Allied prisoners of war once it was learned where the prison camps were located. Admiral Halsey directed Admiral Badger to move his "Flag" to the *USS San Diego* and to take necessary action to set up preparations for Occupation and Surrender Day. General Douglas MacArthur would be the presiding Officer conducting the Surrender Ceremony for the Allied Forces on the *USS Missouri.* (BB 38)

When an Admiral's "Flag" is coming aboard it means that his staff of 25 Officers and 75 enlisted men need to be provided bedding, blankets and cots from other ships. In addition, there is need for more typewriters, mimeograph machines, paper and general office supplies and not to forget the need for more food provisions and general supplies. In addition to solving these needs the situation is further complicated because 80 of the San Diego crew were in training as a landing force. Further demands on the San Diego's crew was the urgent need for an additional 100 men to act as a police force.

Background by L. Peter Wren:

Before the *USS San Diego* could enter Tokyo Bay it was necessary to have the US Mine Sweepers sweep Sagami Bay which precedes Tokyo Bay. Following the Mine Sweepers would be several US Destroyers whose job it would be to sink the mines once they floated to the surface. Sagami Bay as well as many Japanese Bays were mined by American airplanes that dropped mines to help put a strangle hold on Japanese shipping during the war. Once Sagami Bay was declared clear the *USS San Diego* and the other US vessels could safely enter Tokyo Bay.

For those readers who are not acquainted with fleet operations let me offer an overview. Operating with a large Task Forces, Destroyers perform many assignments and are called "Small Boys." They are sent to escort, to investigate a potential problem, to assist in recovering a downed pilot, to search the sea for enemy submarines and to sink floating mines, to deliver mail to small outposts, as well as movies. These duties are many and well handled. Destroyers check things out and report back to the "Big Boys." Destroyers are also called "Tin Cans" because they do not have any extra hull protection and are also called "Greyhounds of the Sea" because of their speed and maneuverability.

Colonel Lewis Held, Quartermaster., Gen MacArthur's Staff:

With Occupation Day being organized it was interesting to learn the following information from Colonel Lewis I. Held, US Army, of Richmond, Virginia. Colonel Held was in charge of the Quartermaster Staff for General MacArthur. MacArthur knew of the treachery of the Japanese War Lords from experience. If there was to be any treachery it would be wise to prepare for it. To be on the safe side of entering Tokyo, he directed Colonel Held to locate 1,000 parachutes for a possible parachute jump into the Tokyo airport in order to seize the airport area. Once the airport was seized the American forces could land a larger invasion force to bring about the surrender. The treachery did not occur and the surrender was accomplished without incident. Colonel Held reported the parachutes were ready, though very difficult to accumulate in such a short period of time, and thankfully not needed.

LT. Frank Heald Continues:

When the *USS San Diego* docked along side the Japanese Naval Base in Yokosuka the ship was host to large group of American senior officers. Yokosuka is a seaport just south of Yokohama and Tokyo and the first seaport prior to entering the Tokyo Bay. In addition to Fleet Admirals Chester Nimitz and Bill Halsey, General Robert Eichelberger (8th Army), and Major General Roy S. Geiger, US Marine Corps, there were several more lesser ranked Admirals and Generals now all on the main deck of the *USS San Diego*. Frank Heald had many photo-ops and his work most likely can be found in the Naval Archives, College Park, Maryland.

Departing the Yokosuka Naval Base everything seemed to fall into place when the *USS San Diego* arrived in

Yokohama, the seaport just south of Tokyo. For security reasons against possible Japanese treachery there was plenty of air power flying above the *USS San Diego* from US Naval Carriers.

The Japanese Battleship *Nagato* was a wreck and lay just off port side and hardly afloat. The *USS San Diego* was probably closer to her than any other ship since December 7, 1941 and was the first ship to anchor in Tokyo Bay. Many correspondents and commentators were describing the event with all the airwaves going to Guam for further routing to the United States.

Imperial Japanese Ship	United States Ship
Nagato August '45	*Nagato* August '45
Tokyo Bay 12:00 noon	Tokyo Bay 12:10 noon

On the 29th of August the *USS Missouri* and the *USS Iowa* steamed into Tokyo Bay and dropped anchor. Admiral Halsey was aboard the *USS Missouri*. Now high rankings of all kinds began to appear. Navy Commander Harold Stassen—a presidential hopeful, came aboard to help plan the evacuation of Prisoners of War. Brigadier General William Clement, USMC, was in charge of the first stages of the landing forces. Correspondence men and cameramen were everywhere.

The *USS San Diego*'s highlight was when the "ship's prize crew," in a motor whale boat, boarded the Imperial Japanese Naval (IPN) vessel *Nagato* and hauled down the Rising Sun flag and then a few minutes later ran up the American Flag to the peak of the mast. Admiral Badger aboard the *USS San Diego* sent a message to Admiral Halsey on the *USS Missouri*, "Japanese flag struck on IPN *Nagato*. American Flag hoisted on *USS Nagato*."

More Background:

Two Japanese Officers, who will be interpreters, were being transferred to the *USS San Diego* from a Destroyer in Tokyo Bay by "high-line." For explanation a high-line is a sturdy hawser stretched between two ships on which a trolley block rides. Attached to the trolley is an open seat called a "Boatswain's Chair" in which the person being transferred sits and dangles his feet over the water space between the ships. Attached to the Boatswain Chair are two lines. (A line is in layman's terms is a rope.) One is used to pull the seat toward the other ship and one is used to return the seat back to the originating ship. Both ships must maintain the course and speed as deck hands keep the transfer line taut. The originating ship, by manpower slacks off line if the ships vary in course steering, and takes up slack when the ships tend to veer together. In transferring in rough seas it is difficult and occasionally the transferee does get a saltwater dip. Ship's crews are very careful when transferring a wounded or an ill shipmate. In this case the sick or wounded are placed in a wire basket (Stokes Stretcher) rather than the seat. The Deck Officer and his crew have control of the safe transfers.

LT. Frank Heald Continues:

In this transfer, the *San Diego*'s ship Officer prevailed on the line handlers to keep the line taut and the Japanese Officers arrived dry on the deck of the *San Diego*. Upon the arrival of the Japanese Officers, one of the ship's crew after seeing how short they were, was heard to mutter, "Hell, is that what we are fighting? We'd throw that shrimp size back in the States!"

Japanese Officers would also come out to the *USS San Diego* anchorage by small boat and come aboard via the Quarterdeck gangway. On these occasions the Boatswain of the Watch was instructed to frisk them. Any gun or knife weapons found were to be taken and put in safekeeping and would be returned when they were departing. Security of the ship and its crew was paramount and there was a natural feeling that they might become treacherous while on board.

On one occasion when one of the larger Boatswain mates was on duty a Japanese Officer and his interpreter came to the top of the gangway for boarding. The "Boatswain mate" frisked him, finding no weapon, slipped his hands under the armpits of the Japanese Officer, picked him up and placed him gently on the deck. Then "Boatswain Mate" signaled to the interpreter and repeated the same procedure. After being escorted to where he was supposed to go on the San Diego, and fully out of hearing the Quarterdeck Watch crew burst-out in a hearty laugh.

In Explanation:

The Japanese Nationals would not know the procedure for coming aboard the ship, such as saluting the Quarter-deck Officer and requesting permission to step off the gang-way on to the ship. The first visitor, not speaking English needed all the help he could get. The second visitor was the interpreter and though he spoke English, he too didn't know the procedure. The Boatswain Mate did what he thought was the easiest way to welcome them so he used the "under the arm" method.

LT. Frank Heald Continues:

On another occasion a Japanese Officer, who was Com-mandant of the Yokohama Navy Yard came aboard. He was a very short pudgy fellow with three rows of ribbons on his uniform and wearing white gloves. Behind him was a civilian interpreter. He arrived without appointment and through his interpreter announced the purpose of his visit was to surrender the Yokohama Navy Yard to the American Naval Forces. Unfortunately he was made to wait on the Quarterdeck for at least 15 minutes before the proper mili-tary scene could be arranged for Admiral R. B. Carncy, (Halsey's Chief of Staff) to receive the surrender. Admiral Badger, skipper of the *San Diego* accompanied Admiral Carney who accepted the surrender of the Yokohama Navy Yard in Halsey's behalf. The ceremony was very short. A few words were spoken, and then repeated in English by the interpreter, followed by the presentation of a letter to Admiral Carney. Thus control of the Naval base was now in American hands.

LT. Frank Heald Continues:

Frustration starts with the letter "F" as in Frank's first name. Here he is aboard the *USS San Diego* and docked along side of a Japanese Navy Yard. It is just a few steps down the dock to the Main Gate which will give Frank a chance to see a little of Japan and perhaps purchase a small souvenir. But urgent messages keep him anchored to the ship's communication shack as he battles with communications of every possible nature. Two days later the word comes to stand by to receive about 300 men and officers who are eligible for the "Magic Carpet." This is a transfer home. The Main Gate takes a suddenly lower priority when the word "Homeward Bound" boldly and blaringly comes from the decoding machine's humming in the Radio Shack. What can you say to that decoded message? The answer is simple and easy. Thank you Lord, and God Bless America!

Source: Letter from Lieut. Franklin Heard.

L. Peter Wren

The Victory Table

It is the day of the Japanese Surrender. We are aboard the Battleship, *USS Missouri* and anchored in Tokyo Bay, Japan. The date is September 2, 1945 and the time is 0600 am. Chow (breakfast) has been completed. The sweepers have manned their brooms and are making ready for the formal surrender of the Japanese to the Allied Forces. Some of the dignitaries are aboard and many others will be arriving. In the distance, there is a slight fog hanging just below the well-shaped peak of Mount Fuji. The Tokyo Bay is dripping with US Naval and Allied shipping and a few ships are underway to a distant but designated anchorage site. On the *USS Missouri* the American flag, two blocked at the peak of the main mast, fluttering proudly in the morning breeze. Seagulls call raucously, protesting the many ships crowding their sea resting places.

USS Missouri, Battleship (BB63) is being escorted by two USS Fletcher Class Destroyers into Tokyo Bay prior to the surrender of Japan scheduled for September 2, 1945.
Japanese Mount Fugi is in the background.
This picture is the work of David McComb of Bolton Landing, NY who graciously permitted its use.

The Quarterdeck is the first place of reception, and resounds with the Boatswains piping and commands for side boys saluting. The ship's bell continues to give notice by six or eight bells of the arrival of more Senior Officers and dignitaries. Escorts usher Admirals, Generals and ranking others to proper assembly place on the *USS Missouri*. The Boatswain wipes the morning mists from the polished brass leading to the ceremony area, where all will witness the final act to close World War II.

Everything is well planned, laid out and coordinated. Nothing has been overlooked, or astray. The ship's crew are comfortably waiting for the ceremony to start. Some enlisted men have climbed high on the ship's structure claiming to each other, that they have the best seat to observe this glorious moment.

Then fifteen minutes before the ceremony is to begin the Admiral's Aide brings out the documents to be signed. With a bewildered look he asks, "Where is the table on which to place these surrender papers?" Everyone in earshot stops and looks at the puzzled Aide, who, if his hands were not full of documents could also have scratched his head as they had done.

It is true that the First Lieutenant is responsible for all deck spaces on this ship. It is a good question and it is repeated again. "Where is the table?" Well, all sailors know we do not have portable tables aboard ship. Because heavy seas are often encountered and all equipment must securely installed or triced up to remain in place when the ship is caught in the "dip, and the roll and the pitch of a heavy wave." If things are not securely placed they become flying missiles respecting no one as they sail from bulkhead to bulkhead. "Watch out" and "Duck" are the common words that are heard!

Well, the Boatswain mate disappears from that area and after a short period, he is back with a mess hall table from the crew's mess. The Officer's steward brings the green tablecloth and covers the worn and heavily used mess table which now takes a sturdy stand with the surrender papers in place. The crew up in the rigging having recognized the table, are pointing, clapping their hands in glee and saying, "That's 'OUR' table!"

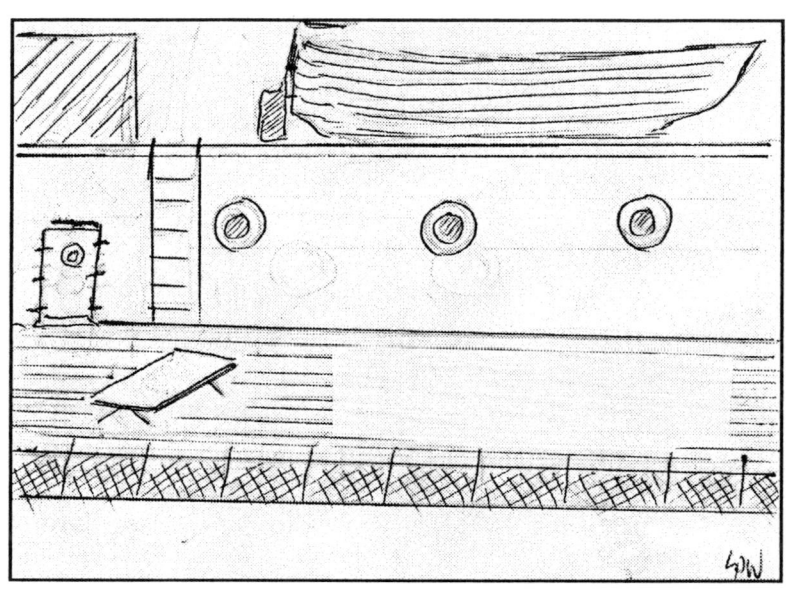

A ship's crew mess table awaiting a cover and the surrender papers at 0800 hours September 2, 1945 aboard the *USS Missouri* in Tokyo Bay.

Then the parade of rank begins as places are taken. The Japanese surrender officials stand off to the right and shift back and forth on their short stubby legs. There are many ribboned and medal bedecked Admirals, Generals, Colonels, Captains and Commanders at this ceremony. Many have a part to play others are just observers. There is much pomp and circumstance being performed and observed. But when all is said and done, the greatest act performed was by that of the lowly mess hall table. The signing of the surrender could not have been completed without this highly used wooden mess table. It has performed a very valuable and honorable service for this occasion. Like all sailors, it too receives a set of shipping orders. Its destination is to the halls of a Naval Academy building in Annapolis, Maryland where it will continue to stand as evidence of a Victory. We will summarize this table story by saying, "They also serve who only stand and wait!"

By: L. Peter Wren LCDR USNR (ret)

Winter clothing for Korea
(See page 183)

Occupation Kure, Japan
Jack Paul's Memoirs

Jack Paul was my shipmate on the *USS Bassett* and was an LCVP crewman working very closely with the landing of American Army troops. He like the rest of us was apprehensive as to what to expect from the Japanese Nationals, though the war was over.

He writes:

The *USS Bassett* was loaded with a contingent of US Army troops to be transported to Kure, Japan for the purpose of placing American Occupational troops at their large Kure Naval Base located on the Inland Sea. The city of Kure, is just south of the atom bombed city of Hiroshima.

The American troops prior to boarding the Bassett were veterans of Pacific campaigns and were to be rotated States side when they received new orders directing them to this new assignment. Naturally they were not thrilled with this situation, but coming aboard the *USS Bassett* they found more amenities than they had seen since they left the United States. First there were showers with fresh hot water. Second there were no foxholes to be dug, and third there were three prepared meals every day on a regular schedule, with coffee pots brewing fresh "Joe" for these G.I. Joes. Snacks were also available and desserts with every meal. No need to eat those dried rations or boil anything in you helmet. Powdered milk fresh from a chilled refrigeration system plus scrambled eggs every morning was like eating in a first class French restaurant. They concluded the Navy knew how to fight a war. Thank God for the calm waters of the Inland Sea because there was no seasickness as we plowed the waters between the homeland islands of Honsho and Shikoku. Every Army man had his own clean bunk and there was no K.P. [Kitchen Police] details for our US Army guests.

We left Wakayama, Japan on 4 October and sailed for the Kure Naval Base about 330 miles away. Upon arrival we dropped anchor among other US Naval vessels and awaited instructions as to when we would move our Army guests to their new location. The *USS Bassett* is designated as a "Fast Troop Transport" and has the four LCVPs aboard for putting an armed force ashore quickly. An LCVP is a Landing Craft able to transport both a Vehicle and Personnel. As we swung on the hook awaiting orders we observed two things. First there were many Japanese vessels sunk in the immediate area, and second we observed a Japanese launch leaving their Naval base and heading for one of the large USS vessels also swinging on the hook. [anchored]. The Japanese dignitaries disappeared aboard the American ship and we presumed that the arrangements were being made as to the US Army take over.

Watching from the bridge of our ship, on the long glass [large binoculars] we saw the Japanese Delegation reappear and their launch headed back to their Naval Base. The *Bassett's* boat crews were now along side and loading our Army guests for a landing on the shores of the Japanese Naval Base. As the LCVPs made their way toward the beach there was concern and apprehension that perhaps some of the militant and die hard Japanese would try something to disrupt the occupation. Our LCVP crews ran the vessels up on the beach and lowered the ramps. The Army personnel disembarked and formed up on the Naval Base awaiting further orders. There appeared to be no problems so the LCVPs were ordered back to the *USS Bassett.*

From the bridge the *Bassett* crew watched the Japanese lower their War Flag, fold it up and march off to one side of the field. The US Army contingent then proceeded to raise the American Flag on the same pole which was then followed by all the American troops saluting it. Then the Japanese senior officer came forward, bowed and presented his sword. The US Army senior officer accepted it, thanked the officer, and then handed it right back to him. Having witnessed our first occupational event we were pleased with our helping to secure the peace we all welcomed.

Shipmate Skordahl's story follows and gives an accounting of his experience in visiting the area of Hiroshima

Hiroshima
Vernon Skordahl Rides Shot Gun

When the *USS Bassett* finished escorting a large group of LCMs to the area of Kure, Japan the ship was very close to the area of the Hiroshima bombing. Skordahl was assigned to a Shore Patrol team to direct the Japanese truck drivers to a specific warehouse in the area of the LCVP landing docks. Skordahl said it was like in the "Old West Movies" in that the shore patrol was riding escort {shot gun} with their Japanese drivers to make sure they went to the correct warehouse. The cargo was a very large amount of Japanese rifles and swords which were being put under United States control.

When the shore party arrived at the assignment area, they noted that they were on the edge of where the Hiroshima bomb was dropped. The Japanese civilian workers were all wearing cloth facemasks which covered their nose and mouth. The shore patrol did not receive any type of cloth mask and became concerned. The ground was covered with a gray white powder which as one walked about in it became an air borne dust which they were inhaling. Their shoes and leggings were beginning to collect the gray powder. No effort was made to provide the shore patrol with protective masks.

Looking in toward the center of the area, Skordahl said there seemed to be a saucer like depression that was full of rubble. The foundations of building and homes were slightly visible. He said you could see a few railings and steps leading up to a building. The area was very flat and the gray white dust seemed to be everywhere. There weren't any landmarks so it was hard to judge distance. He thought the center was about 5 to 6 miles away. It could have been more.

They mounted the loaded trucks with the Japanese drivers and with the maps provided, directed the drivers by sign language to the landing dock warehouses. After several trips on the trucks, Skordahl and his shore patrol buddies were getting bored with the same dirty road and flat area. Since the drivers knew the route to the warehouses they put them under their own cognizance and let them make the trips on their own. They walked around the area but there wasn't much to see so they proceeded to the meeting area for transport back to the LCVP boat docks.

The next day Skordahl drew the shore patrol assignment again and after a short meeting with his group, they sent the Japanse drivers on their rounds without escort. The shore patrol did not receive facemasks on the second day and were concerned about their exposure to the radiation from the atomic bombing. With no protection provided and since the Japanese drivers were performing what was expected of them without the escort, the shore patrol group took a short tour of the area and then gathered up a few of the guns and swords for their friends who had the duty aboard the ship and would not be near this source of souvenirs

The Bassett departed the area and put into the harbor near Nagasaki where Skordahl drew a shore patrol assignment again. This time he refused to obey the orders of his division officer. He was given a Captains Mast, which is a form of a hearing of the case by the ship's Captain, and with proper punishment meted to the offender of the rules. Skordahl was given 100 hours of extra duty and confined to the ship until it was completed. The boatswain mate was to see that the punishment was carried out and when completed report back to the Captain. While Skordahl doesn't talk about it, but it is rumored that Skordahl had an easy time with the boatswain because of the nice sword he had purloined for the boatswain before the ship left the Hiroshima.

Skordahl is in his seventies and reports he is enjoying good health in spite of his exposure in Hiroshima. Shortly after his phone call I learned Vernon Skordahl died.

Source: Phone call (April 1999) from Vernon S. Skordal— a *USS Bassett* shipmate.

Prisoners of War Freed
Geo. R. Clark's Story

The following is an interesting letter I gleaned from the book by George L. Clark entitled *An Illustrated History of the USS Cockrell DE 366*. George has granted me permission to use it to tell the true stories of Japanese brutality to Prisoners of War. This letter is from a shipmate on the *USS Cockrell* to his wife and family. This letter relates more of what POWs suffered under the Japanese brutality. Also there is a good description of the general destruction of Japanese towns and cities received from allied bombings.

THE LETTER

Saturday 15 Sept 1945
Wakayama, Japan

Dear Family:

On Thursday morning I was called and told to collect my paints and brushes and report to an aircraft carrier within an hour. I did so and was introduced to another sign writer (Jewish) and we were told to go over to the hotel on the shore. It seems that the POW's were scheduled to arrive from the camps on Friday morning and the Navy had taken over the hotel as a delousing and embarkation center. Now to describe that hotel.

It is a seashore resort hotel and its name translated means "The Hotel of a Thousands Waves." It is impossible for me to pronounce, or even spell it in Japanese. It was constructed entirely of wood and all inlays. All doors were of the sliding type and where the use of frosted glass was needed, they used rice paper instead. A fuller description will have to be given verbally. Each room in the hotel was designated as an office, such as—Emergency Hospital, Dental Clinic, Records, War crimes Complaints and etc. Our job was to make signs over the doors so that prisoners would know what was where. We worked from about 2pm to about 4 pm and finished most of them. The officer in charge told us we could tour the town of Wakanoura in the locality of the hotel. Wakayama was the next town. We walked through the narrow streets and we were as much a curiosity to them as they were to us. We weren't allowed to loiter. We covered the town in about an hour and the minutia details will have to wait until I can describe them verbally.

At 6pm I went by barge to my ship and imagine my surprise when I learned my ship had left on a mission. I had previously been told to come back the next day as there were more signs to be made. I spoke to the officer in charge and he said he'd radio my ship to let them know where I was, and that I should sleep on the carrier. The fellow I was with was just marvelous (the Jewish fellow). He got me my supper, a cot to sleep on and towels and soap to take a shower. In the morning (5:30 am) he took me into the kitchen and made us steak and eggs for breakfast. We went back to the hotel at 6:30 am and made signs until about 9:00 am.

Now starts the most exciting and heart touching experience of my entire life. I was assigned to ride in a truck which was to go to the railroad station at Wakayama to meet the first train load of Allied prisoners coming from the prison camps. It was my job to see that the Japanese driver did not turn off anywhere and to go straight to the station. We rode through the "Residential" section of Wagayama. I wrote that in quotes as the homes were nothing but unpainted boards and bamboo thrown together. The people were in rags and most wore wooden dongs. Next we rode through the industrial section, if you could call the ten or so square miles of rubbish, broken glass and bricks an industrial area. Yep, the B-29's had made a three hour incendiary bomb raid on July 9, 1945. The ruin was devastating and made me proud as hell at the magnificent job of precision bombing. The station itself was metal and huge gaping holes in the roof attested to the terrific pasting it took. One track was repaired so as to facilitate the transport of prisoners.

At 10:00 am the welcoming party was all assembled. These included nurses, Red Cross people, a British Band, and a battery of official photographers, cameramen and your husband. The train pulled in a few minutes later and I am not ashamed to admit that tears rolled down my cheeks. I wasn't alone so I didn't feel conspicuous in my extreme happiness. The men leaned out of the windows laughing, shouting, and crying. The majority were able to walk but there were some stretcher cases which were rushed to waiting ambulances to be transported as soon as possible to the hospital ships. The rest were loaded into our trucks and brought back to our hotel where again they were welcomed. This time by the officials and a large Navy band.

The men were then started on a regular routine through the hotel. As near as possible this is a rough idea of what they went through. First they were stripped of all their clothes and were sprayed with DDT, a delousing powder. Next they took showers and were sprayed personally with the same powder. From there they were examined by the doctors and the worst cases were assigned to the hospital ships. The others were sent to the various ships for transportation to Guam, Okinawa or other separation centers. From these centers they would be sent to the countries from whence they came. The largest percentage was Dutch and the rest were British, Canadian and Yanks. Practically all were in prison three years. Later on in this "book" I will devoted more time to the conditions under which these men existed, but not lived, in the prison camps.

My next job was to escort groups of ten down to the landing docks which would take them to the ships in the harbor. I see re-reading I omitted a very important stage in the routine at the hotel. One room was set aside for the expressed purpose of obtaining from the men all information which would assist the Army in punishing those "Yellow Bastards" who mistreated the men while they were imprisoned. They were satisfied even to get nicknames of the war criminals. A big sign in the room where the men were questioned read, "You give us the details and we know what to do with them."

All the men were in excellent spirits and talked freely to us. No atrocity movie could portray what I heard. At times I could not repress a shudder and too often I almost choked on the lump in my throat. To accurately put those words down on paper would take somebody with greater writing skill as a writer than I am. All I will try to do is to give you the highlights or should I say the lowlights. Magnify these in your mind and then perhaps you will get a small conception of the barbarian tactics of these stupid captors with buckteeth. Imagine grown men existing on one pint a day of a mixture of rice and barley for three years. One cigarette a day if they were "good" which was forfeited for three or four days if a POW misbehaved. Christmas Day was no different as far as food was concerned except that they begged the orange peels from the Japanese children, which they boiled with some birdseed they picked up from the ground and made a sort of a dessert from it. While on the subject of food, imagine if you can this incident. Some of the prisoners were being transported from Thailand to Japan. They sailed in a Jap Cargo vessel and were sealed in a hold. Occasionally, they were thrown some slop. Their huge hunger became so great, with no control over their stomachs they caught flies which were in abundance and ate them. This lasted 78 days.

In the prison camps they worked in metal mills or in aluminum or copper mines. Besides having guards, small Japanese children were given pieces of iron pipe and whenever they felt like it they would swing freely at the POWs. Imagine grown men having to take such abuse from children. Another pastime was to have a guard call a POW to attention and then slap his face until he tired of the sport.

Hearing these stories upset me and writing about them makes my blood boil. I hope I am conveying to you one prime thought. What I am referring to is that we should thank God that He granted us Victory over such a despicable race of people. The men I saw had guts to be able to go through what they did and come up smiling. I know damn well I couldn't have.

I worked continuously from 6 am to 12 midnight yesterday through a terrific downpour. I was soaked through and through. All I ate all day, or should I say drank all day was coffee. As uncomfortable as I was and thoroughly exhausted I enjoyed every minute of it and the sight if these men with legs and arms the thickness of broom handles drove any thought of my tiredness from my mind.

To hit upon a lighter vein while riding the truck with the Japanese driver (who couldn't understand a word of English), I cursed him roundly using words that I never realized existed in my vocabulary. This dirty monkey just grinned and bowed to me while I was doing it and it took an effort to keep myself from slanting his teeth inward instead of out. I didn't though, as the satisfaction of riding through Japan with the thought that we had "Won the War," and the thought with God's help, we would keep these slimy wretches from repeating their atrocities upon civilized nations, was enough to keep me buoyed up.

If I write much more I will have to send this by package rather than by letter. If the War wasn't over you might get the impression that this is "War Bond Propaganda." It is propaganda, propaganda against ever letting such a thing ever happening again.

Sel, honey, I have purposely omitted my usual endearments. I want you to let anyone read this who wishes to. Make those people read it who were constantly griping about rationing and home front difficulties. Another reason was those poor fellows haven't seen or heard from their families in over three years. My mind at present dwells on their happy reunion. Never again will I complain about receiving mail from you. The prisoners were allowed 25 words per month in their letters with no guarantee of delivery and no incoming mail.

I will close now dearest wife by saying that I never could express my feelings to my wife in 25 words. Keep well, darling. I am fine and as usual can't wait to get home.

Love

xxxx

Sights and Sounds of War Torn Japan
Colonel Lewis I. Held, US Army

Colonel Held, who was in charge of supplies for General MacArthur's Army needs, did not leave Manila for Japan until late October 1945. As the seaplane approached the main Island of Honshu the pilot pointed out the snow capped peak of Mt. Fuji. Quite often stratus nimbus clouds lay beneath the peak. This was a cloudless day and Fuji was a beautiful sight to see. Flying into Toyko from the south and over the seaport Yokohama gave the Colonel a chance to see the devastation caused by the American's fire bombing. He wondered why the Japanese people held out so long when every night, since establishing the airfields on Tinian Island, the B-29's fire bombed Japan.

At this time and while stationed in Japan, there were several interesting experiences which Colonel Held shares with his reader. For example, while driving from Tokyo to Kyoto he stopped his army vehicle to ask a young woman for directions. He pulled out his Japanese dictionary and started to ask his question, when the young woman asked in perfect English saying, "*Colonel, can you tell me whether the University of Southern California is still standing?*" She had been a student there and the Japanese propaganda had been claiming that they had leveled the whole U.S. West Coast. Colonel Lewis assured her the University was still standing.

On another October 1945 occasion in Tokyo he was dining with several Allied Officers plus a Russian Captain. The Russian Captain, who spoke good English, commented that he was sorry he had to leave Tokyo because he had to return to Russia for "winter maneuvers." Col. Held inquired, "*My God man, the war is over! Who are you preparing to fight?*" The Captain looked him straight in the eye and answered, "*I am surprised you have to ask?*" (Note: The Russians did not join the Allies' war effort on Japan only after the Nagasaki bomb was dropped on Aug 9, 1945. Japan surrendered 5 days later)

The Cold War between Russia and U.S. had already begun. Here is the background. Truman had feared Russian expansion of Communism in the Far East, and for that reason, demanded that Stalin permit "a short U.S. occupation zone" south of the 38th latitude parallel so American Forces could help Korea recover from the Japanese Invasion. Stalin conceded and MacArthur sent the 24th Corps into the territory. It was Colonel Held's duty to supply warm winter clothing to the Army troops now in Korea. There was no such clothing in the South Pacific tropics at that time.

As other US Army groups were being withdrawn from Europe winter clothing was becoming more available from that theater. Colonel Held, through the communication system, contacted The US Air Force and US ships in the Atlantic Ocean and some in Panama Canal requesting the winter clothing be forwarded to Korea.

On October 31, 1945 Colonel Held flew to Korea to inspect how the 24th American troops were weathering the winter conditions. Winter clothing, housing and food were up to Army standards. As an additional note Communist North Korea invaded South Korea on June 25, 1950 and the writer of this book was recalled to Naval service in January 1,1951.for another tour of duty. Destroyer personnel are always in demand in the Task Forces Operations.

Sixty Days After the Hiroshima Bomb

After the brief inspection of the 24th Army Division in Korea, Colonel Held was en route to Japan by airplane when a passenger needed urgent medical attention. A medical emergency landing was made at the Hiroshima Airport because it had the nearest U.S. Field Hospital. The US Field Hospital was placed in this area to be of medical service to survivors of the bomb and also to offer medical help to our own troops serving in this area.

Being an unexpected landing Colonel Held decided to take a jeep ride around the perimeter of the site where the first bomb was dropped sixty days ago. The terrain was still radioactive but since the bomb was burst in mid air about 2000 feet above the ground there was less hazardous radioactivity and the motored trip was approved. The ground area was reduced to rubble. All that was visible were the many two or three steps for entering homes that no longer existed. The foundations outlined the shape of the former homes and contained metal plumbing pipes, small iron radiators, and electrical wires scattered over the house floor area still covered with rubble. On the concrete slabs of larger buildings and still standing were silhouettes of people etched on the concrete walls. It was as though a photographic negative was made by the flash of the atomic explosion.

In different wards of the U.S. Field Hospital, Japanese adults and children were being fully and carefully treated for their flash burns and wounds. Where the children wore white clothing there was clear normal flesh. Wherever a black garment was worn, severe burns followed the outline of that black clothing. On one man who wore a white shirt with a black tie, the burn was the same shape as the tie he wore.

Source: All items taken from *Lewis I. Held Family History*, Volume 2 by his son Lewis I. Held, Jr. PhD. of Richmond, Va.

Being Welcomed
Ensign L. Peter Wren USNR

The *USS Bassett* was part of the transportation ships that placed the occupation troops in the many locations of Japan. This gave the Bassett crew opportunity to visit various Japanese ports. In going ashore in Japan we received instructions from Naval Headquarters to the effect, that the war was over and not to take or attempt to take any vengeance on the local people. Most of us felt we did not need to be told this and were delightfully surprised at the welcoming receptions upon landing.

The Japanese greeting us were the "momma sans and poppa sans" who are the grandparents minding the grandchildren. Those Japanese of a "war age" were nowhere in sight. The grandmothers and grandfathers bowed graciously to us while the children danced, smiled and sang happy Japanese sounding songs. The children were great ambassadors as they made us feel very welcomed. None of us could resist the cute, happy children and when the grandparents saw our happy reaction to the children greater smiles and greetings emanated from the elder citizens. They knew we came as friends not conquerors.

Many years later I discussed this welcome with my good friend now General Held. It was then that he told me of his earlier experience in the early days of the occupation. While in a motor convoy from Tokyo to Osaka the Japanese citizens walking along the road would turn their backs on the convoy as it passed. He learned later that this was a sign of deep embarrassment for the war.

Chapter Eight

President Truman's Decision

Hashimoto's Letter

Post Script

Addendum
The *USS Missouri* Revisited

President Truman's Decision

In the years following the end of WW II, there are those critics who strongly feel the bombing of the Hiroshima and Nagasaki was an unnecessary, and an uncalled-for action. Sixty years have passed since the world was introduced to the destructive power of the atom bomb. The intelligence known then, is now available to the lay person. Given here is a summary of the facts on which President Truman predicated his decision.

The Casualties

(1) The number of Americans killed or wounded in the European war which included Germany, Italy, the Low lands, Normandy and the African desert, plus those losses from the Pacific Islands including Pearl Harbor, Guadacanal, Tarawa, Kwajalein, Corregidor. Bataan, Palau, Iwo Jima and Okinawa, all weighed heavily on President Truman. Let's not forget Harry Truman served in World War One and knew well the causalities of WW One. He knew well the lines of the poem by John McCrae—1872-1918

"In Flanders Field, the poppies blow,
Between the crosses, row on row."

The Youth

(2) With the establishment of the women's corps of WAVES and WACs, Truman knew more young American males would be on the battle lines. He also knew the United States was now drafting the 18 year olds. Many of the 17 year olds were joining up with their parent's permission. Since European Battles were over many of these American teen-age youths were being transferred to the Pacific war.

The ships and aircraft are now being manned by the 17-18 and 19 teenagers. Those who served then are now the 77, 78 and 79 year old veterans of 2005

German Atomic Progress

(3) With the German War over in early May 1945, Truman learned the German scientists were heavily engaged in the development of an "Atomic Bomb." President Truman also knew there were German Scientists who did not want Hitler to have the atomic bomb. He also knew German scientists were sharing their atomic progress with Japan. He learned Germany had not been successful in producing a bomb

Japan—Uranium Oxide

(4) Japan had an edge on a bomb's development because of the location of uranium oxide. When Japan invaded Korea they discovered an adequate source of uranium oxide in a mining area. Two of the rivers which flow into the Yalu River were dammed to develop a turbo-electric power plant. This plant was able to separate the oxide from the uranium. Now the problem was to enrich the uranium to create a bomb. (**Note:** A problem still exists today with North Korea as their leadership announced in 2005 that they now possessed an "A" bomb. Why does North Korea need it? Now that they possess the bomb how and where will they use it?) This is a question of great concern.

A Nova Scotia Surrender

(5) In April 1945 (a month before the surrender), "a special equipped German submarine" departed Germany en route to Japan with supplies and equipment to further

the Japanese atomic project. Shortly after its departure Germany surrendered and recalled all military sea units (ships, raiders and submarines) back to Germany. The skipper of "a special German Submarine" elected to surrender to the Allied Forces in Halifax, Nova Scotia rather than return to Germany. The details of this submarine's voyage and cargo to Japan were known to President Truman. (See the book—*The Last Great Secret of the Third Reich* by Arthur O. Naujoks & Lee Nelson, Issued 2002)

Surrender—Not an Option

(6) The Potsdam terms of surrender were accepted by Germany and Italy on May 07,1945. **V-E Day** was celebrated on May 8th 1945. The terms were then presented to Japan to also comply with the Potsdam provisions. Japanese philosophy taught surrender was not an honorable choice. This is illustrated several times in this book. The Japanese delayed in 1945 through the balance of May, June, July and half of August. Perhaps they believed in those 99 days they could achieve an atomic bomb to defeat the Allied Invasion of their home islands. The Japanese Military command delayed surrender even though American forces on Okinawa were but 350 miles from their southern most island. American nightly bombing missions from Tinian and Iwo Jima were followed by daytime flights to see the effects of the night bombs and set new targets for the next night's bombing flights. It was getting to the point where there was little left to bomb. Yet there was no surrender as this was not an honorable choice in their philosophy.

Australian & British Fleets En Route to Tokyo

(7) The British and the Australian Navies were now joining with the American Forces for the invasion of Japan.

The Japanese Military could monitor the airwave traffic and know it was just a matter of time before the Allied landing would soon come. Perhaps they thought their atomic bomb was nearer to completion and they could again see a "Great Wind" come and destroy the Allied fleet off its shores as a "wind" (Typhoon) did when they were threatened by the Chinese Navy many years ago.

The Clock is Ticking:
   Germany surrenders May 7, 1945
   V-E Day celebrated May 8, 1945
   Potsdam Agreement issued to Japan
   30 days later—June 7th—no answer from Japan
   60 days later—July 7th—no answer from Japan
   70 days later—July 16th—Bomb loaded on *USS Indy*
   80 days later—July 26th—bomb arrives Tinian Island
   90 days later—Aug 5th—bomb loaded on Enola Gay
   91 days later—Aug 6th —Hiroshima bombed
   94 days later—Aug 9th—Nagasaki bombed
   99 days later—Aug 14th—Japan surrenders

USS Indianapolis **Tragedy—Sunk at 0041 Hours on 7-30-1945.**

(8) When 60 days had passed and the Potsdam Provisions were not accepted by Japan, President Truman authorized "the bombs" be rushed to Tinian Island. This date would be the16th of July when the *USS Indy* departed San Francisco with an unknown cargo in a black box. Ten days later (July 26th) the unknown cargo was unloaded on Tinian Island. No response from Japan. Ten days later on August 5th the decision was made to bomb Hiroshima. Still no response from Japan. The unknown black box item was loaded on the Enola Gay with Colonel Paul Tibbetts making delivery on August 6th. No response from Japan. Three

days later (August 9th) the Nagasaki bomb was delivered. No response from Japan. Five days after the Nagasaki bomb on August 14th the Japanese War Lords agreed to the Potsdam Provisions. This was a difficult decision for a warring nation who finally agreed surrender was a better option than total devastation.

The Decision Weighed

(9) The 99 days and the considerations listed are a best estimates of the facts which President Truman carefully weighed. The Japanese scientists were very near the development of their own "A" bomb. Robert K. Wilcox, in his book *Japan's Secret War*, states American intelligence in the Pacific received the shocking report that the Japanese developed and successfully test fired an atomic bomb just prior to their surrender.

The failure to use their bomb was "most likely" due to the lack of an adequate aircraft to deliver the bomb.

Robert Wilcox's book states, "*The Japanese are not solely the victims of the bombs as they have portrayed themselves for so long. They were willing to be participants in its use and are only the losers in the race to develop it.*" The reader is encouraged to get a copy of the book by Arthur O. Naujoks and Lee Nelson, entitled *The Last Great Secret of the Third Reich* for more facts.

Hashimoto's Letter

The reader will think it strange to find in this book a listing of another Japanese National, who was once an enemy warrior. Because of his battle experience, this enemy warrior continues to honor and respect Americans. Also, because of that experience, this one time enemy warrior has disposed of his sword and quickly rose with his pen to aid an American warrior in distress. The act of this Japanese warrior is worth repeating in this book as it gives example of how gentlemen of different Nations should strive to prevent war.

Captain Moschitsura Hashimoto, a Japanese Naval Officer, was in command of the Japanese Submarine I-58 whose torpedoes sunk the *USS Indianapolis* (CA 35). The sinking occurred four days (July 30, 1945) after the atomic bombs were delivered to Tinian Island. The sinking caused the loss of 880 men. Sadly Hashimoto also suffered a great personal loss. His parents, and his brother were residents of Hiroshima, and were lost in that bombing.

Because of the loss of the *USS Indianapolis,* Captain Charles B. McVay, III, USN was Court Martial for hazarding his ship by not zigzagging. Of the 186 US Naval ships sunk during World War II, Captain Charles B. McVay III was the only ship's Captain court-martialed for losing his ship in a war zone. Whereas the loss of one's family in such an explosion is a deep emotional experience, so also is the loss of a ship, a crew and a career of an Naval Academy Officer who followed his father's footsteps into the Navy of his beloved country. .

Captain Hashimoto came to the Court Martial hearing in December 1945 to give evidence in behalf of Captain McVay III. His words were not well received by the Court even though he spoke the truth. Captain McVay III was judged guilty. Had escort vessels been assigned to the *USS*

Indy the sinking, would most likely, not have occurred. Also if proper action would have been undertaken on the missed ETA (estimated time of arrival in Leyte Gulf) the loss of so many lives could have been prevented. Much has been written and said about the Captain Charles B. McVay's Court Martial. There were many errors surrounding the lack of communications that left eight hundred eighty men, who it is believed had successfully abandoned ship, in the Philippine Sea for five nights. Only 317 of the total 1197 men survived. Mochitsura Hashimoto states clearly then and again in his letter below, that he could not have missed sinking the ship. In addition to the load of torpedoes he carried, he also had three "Kaitens" aboard. "Kaitens" are torpedoes launched by a mother submarine and driven by a young Japanese crewmember who has committed himself to suicide for the honor of his country. This type of torpedo attack was part of the Japanese last effort to sink many American ships so the Allied forces could not invade the Japanese Homeland.

The following is his letter to Senator John Warner who was chairman of the Senate Armed Services Committee. Captain Hashimoto, was then age 91 and a Shinto priest in Kyoto. Japan. At age 91, to make a trip to Washington to clear an American Officer's name is indeed a true "patriot's act."

L. Peter Wren

The Letter

24 November 1999

ATTN: The Honorable John W. Warner
Chairman, Senate Armed Service Committee
Russell Office Bldg, Washington, D. C. 20510

I hear that your National Legislature is considering resolutions which would clear the name of the late Charles Butler McVay III, Captain of the *USS Indianapolis* which was sunk on 30 July 1945, by torpedo fired from the submarine which was under my command

I do not understand why Captain McVay was court-martialed. I do not understand why he was convicted on the charge of hazarding his ship by failing to zigzag because I would been able to launch a successful torpedo attack against his ship whether it had been zigzagging or not.

I have met many of your brave men who survived the sinking of the *USS Indianapolis.* I would like to join with them in urging that your National Legislature clear the Captain's name.

Our people have forgiven each other for that terrible war and its consequences. Perhaps it is time for your people to forgive Captain McVay for the humiliation of his unjust conviction.

Sincerely
/s/ (Japanese writing characters)

Mochitsura Hashimoto
Umenomiya Taisha,
30 Fukeno Kawa Machi, Umeau,
UKyo-ku, Kyoto 615-0921, Japan

In 1968, Captain Charles B. McVay III deeply depressed by his beloved Navy's action in 1945, committed suicide. Fifty-six years later, in August 2001, as a result of a review of the Court Martial charges, the Captain's good name was restored, his records expunged and he was promoted (though now deceased) to the rank of Rear Admiral. Captain McVay's son Kimo McVay, who fought to restore his father's name died two weeks before the charges were withdrawn. Charles B. McVay IV, son of Captain Charles B. McVay III, attended the 2001 *USS Indy* reunion and celebrated with the living survivor crewmembers the joy of seeing his father's good name cleared of those unjust charges.

Source: Copy of Hashimoto's ltr to Senator John Warner received while attending 2001 *USS Indy* reunion.

Post Script

In the foreword of this book the narrator suggested the three possible avenues which should be used to settle a dispute, namely by pen, or a book of laws or a debating skill." If these methods fail then it would be deemed necessary to pick up the "tools of war" to resolve the dispute. In the Hiroshima bombing we have seen the results of the "new tool of war." Thinking leaders of Nations would heartily suggest that such power only be used in the future for the good of mankind. Yet, why is it that the threat of war still continues when we have established a leadership body called the United Nations to keep peace among Nations? The **"pen, the book of laws, and debating skills"** are all available to the leaders of the United Nations. Why are they failing?

The Allies offered a **"book of laws"** called the "Potsdam Agreement" to end the war. The European warring nations acquiesced whereas Japan refused and after a 90 day waiting period, the **"new tools of war"** were released on Hiroshima and Nagasaki.

It is sad to note that North Korea continues to ignore **"our penned notes"** asking them why do they feel they need a Nuclear Bomb? It is sad to see the "debating skills" of the United Nations are not effective as a deterrent to North Korea's "Nuclear Quest." The United Nations was instigated and founded by America in 1945 with hope that all future disputes would be settled peacefully. America's illustration of "atomic power" in World War II should be forever a deterrent for all nations to recognize that war through the use of this "new tool" is not the way to settle differences.

It is sad to see the United Nation's so called **"Police Action"** or the " Korean War" which America and other Nations fought in 1950 through 1953 to stop the Communist threat, ended at the 38th parallel where it was started.

Now 52 years later (2005) it appears as though the "**new tools of war**" are not too far in the distant future.

President Ronald Reagan's "**debating skills**" brought down the Communist wall which separated Germany. Where are the United Nation's "**debating skills**" in view of this North Korean nuclear threat? Where is the leadership? America leads the way by being the **originator, the host nation and the largest contributor** toward its purpose.

This narrator closes this book with the hope and prayers that again another patriot will rise and speak just as our President Ronald Reagan did when the walls separating Germany fell and Germany consolidated. On Consolidation Day Germany united the eastern and western halves into one country. On that day this author and his wife, Helen, were in Germany and the joy was unbounded. Would the German people ever forget the American Patriot who was not afraid to apply his "debating skills" in their behalf. Will another "patriot" arise again with "debating skills" from Europe, Asia, the Orient, Africa or America to stem the tide of war? God Bless America for the leadership that has been given to this World

L. Peter Wren

Addendum
The *USS Missouri* Revisited

When the *USS Missouri* (BB63) completed the Japanese surrender in Tokyo Bay, the ship proceeded south to Leyte Gulf in the Philippines to refuel and replenish. Since the war is over the foremost question on all sailor's minds was, "When are we heading back to the States?" Many of the senior shipmates were now eligible for discharge based on point system of the "Magic Carpet."

The reserves who served in the Navy were recruited for the duration of the war (DOW) plus six months. Those who had joined the regular Navy were committed to a tour of four or six years. The magic number for discharge was 50 points. One point was counted for each month of service. Married mates received an automatic 25 points. However a battleship requires many men to continue to be operational. A release is granted for a Stateside trip, if enough points were accumulated and on how quick a replacement would report aboard. It is here that we meet petty officer Gerald Taub who is reporting to the *USS Missouri* as a replacement. This is the story he relates on the *USS Missouri*.

The trip back to the East coast was uneventful. The *USS Missouri*, now in the Atlantic waters, was schedule to "Show the Flag" (make Goodwill Calls) in the Mediterranean Sea. Unfortunately at this time the Turkey Ambassador to America, who resided in Washington, DC became seriously ill and died. His remains were to be shipped to Turkey for burial. The *USS Missouri* was scheduled to make a "Goodwill" call at Constantinople. The ship could easily accommodate American State Department dignitaries and others who were part of the Turkey Embassy. So it was decided to transport the Ambassador's remains and all others by ship back to his homeland. The "Port of Calls" to the other Nations could be made after the internment ceremonies were completed in Turkey. The *USS Missouri*'s size and presence would add more prestige and honors due the deceased Ambassador.

The *USS Missouri* remained in the Constantinople waters for a week receiving warm reception from the Turkish people. Food and lodgings were provided free when the American crewmembers went ashore with one and two day passes. The Turkish Postal System created a new stamp for the occasion bearing the imprint of the *USS Missouri*.

Petty Officer Taub said sailing through the Dardanelles was very interesting. The waterways between the Aegean Sea and the Sea of Marmara is only about three to four miles wide but about forty miles long. After the *USS Missouri* moored, Petty Officer Taub received his first day of "Liberty." This gave him a chance to walk across the bridge which separates Europe from Asia. It is the historic area where Xerxes in 481 BC led an army **WEST** across from Asia to Europe. It is also where Alexander the Great, led an army **EAST** from Europe to Asia. Petty Officer Taub proudly stated, "My foot prints are with the many who have tread this historical path!"

The week in Turkey was pleasant except for one incident. One morning a sailor appeared on the dock. After a few moments delay he started to come aboard without using the proper decorum required when coming aboard an American vessel. The custom requires a salute to the American flag on the stern and then saluting the Officer of the Deck while requesting permission to come aboard. Well, this sailor just walked over the gangway making no attempt to do the proper thing. The Officer of the Deck, noting the rating worn on his uniform, knew the petty officer knew better and queried his lack of respect. This "walk on sailor" did not answer because he was Turkish and didn't speak English. An interpreter from the Port Authority was called to help in this case.

The "walk on sailor" was fully dressed in the American sailor's uniform and upon searching him he also had the wallet of the person whose clothes he was wearing. Well, half of the mystery is solved, but where is the American sailor who is somewhere in Constantinople in his under shorts and barefooted. Did he get "rolled," meaning he had imbibed too much alcohol, passed out and was robbed. Or was he "Drugged" and in a heap in some dark alley of Constantinople? Or did he meet with a fatal accident? Having his wallet the ship knew who the missing mate was. Eventually the local police came to his aid and brought him back to the ship. The "walk-on sailor" was a young Turk who was planning on being a "stow away" aboard the *USS Missouri* for a free trip to the States.

Standard Naval instructions to all shipmates while in foreign ports is to stay in groups. Do not wander off on your own. Even though the poster says, "**Join the Navy and see the World**," it is best not to be seen doing it in your skivvies. "Skivvies" is Navy speech meaning underwear.

Source: Gerald Taub, Richmond, Va.

Index

About the Author

LCDR L. Peter Wren USNR (ret) entered the US Navy on 28 December 1941 and completed "Boot Camp" in Norfolk, Virginia in January 1942. The highest rate earned as an enlisted man was SK 1/c. He was commissioned as a line officer from Columbia University in April 1944 and was assigned to the USS Coates DE 685 in the Atlantic Fleet. He was transferred to the USS Bassett APD 73 in April 1945. On 26 July 1945 the USS Indianapolis delivered the atomic bomb to Tinian Island for later dropping on Hiroshima. The USS INDY was sunk by a Japanese submarine on 30 July 1945 and 159 of the 317 survivors were rescued by the USS Bassett. Wren was a boat officer pulling the survivors from the sea. Wren was released from Naval service in April 1946 and received his degree from Michigan State University in 1948. He was recalled for the Korean War and served on the USS Halsey Powell DD 686 from January 1951 until December 1952. He was released to the Fleet Reserve where he completed 20 plus years of service and retired as a LCDR.

LCDR Wren is a past president of the Richmond, Virginia Council, of US Navy League, and organized the Naval Sea Cadet Program in Richmond, Virginia. He and his wife Helen Morrissey Wren have five children one of whom was a US Navy Doctor.

About the Illustrator/Cover

The cover of this book is the art work of David McComb of Bolton Landing, NY and has been selected because it so poignantly depicts the "Pursuit of Peace." The Man O'War moving across the Pacific Ocean is the *USS Missouri* and leading a mission of peace. The word "Pacific" alone means *"tending toward Peace."*

Whereas Mt Fuji in the background suggests the tip of a war arrow has been severed and peace will now follow in the wake of these vessels as they quietly pass before its majestic height. The *Missouri* is partly hidden by escorting ships whose mission is to carry peace into the shallow waters where the *USS Missouri* can not go but where peace is urgently sought.

In this Work of Art, David McComb, brings the reader to the quick conclusion that the acts of war as written herein should never again be repeated. The book *World War II Revisited* continues the search for Peace.

Printed in the United States
42342LVS00002B/284